CIVIL WAR GENTLEMEN:

1860s Apparel Arts & Uniforms

CIVIL WAR GENTLEMEN:

1860s Apparel Arts & Uniforms

by
R. L. Shep
W. S. Salisbury
With an article by Peter Dervis

Pattern Consultant:
Betty Williams

R. L. Shep
Mendocino

ISBN 0-914046-22-5

Library of Congress #94-37721

Printed in the United States of America

Published by:

    R.L. Shep

    Box 668

    Mendocino, CA 95460

Library of Congress Cataloging-in-Publication Data

Shep, R. L., 1933-
   Civil War gentlemen : 1860's apparel arts & uniforms / by R.L. Shep, W.S. Salisbury, Peter Dervis ; pattern consultant, Betty Williams.
       p.   cm.
   Contains Salisbury's system of actual measurement and drafting for all styles of coats. 1865.
   Includes bibliographical references.
   ISBN 0-914046-22-5 : $24.95
   1. Costume--United States--History--19th century. 2. Men's clothing--United States--History--19th century. 3. Military uniforms--United States--History--19th century. 4. Clothing and dress measurements--United States--History--19th century. 5. United States--Armed Forces--Uniforms--History--19th century. 6. United States--History--Civil War, 1961-1865. 7. United States--Social life and customs--19th century. I. Dervis, Peter, 1963-   .
II. Salisbury, W. S. (Wilbur S.). System of actual measurement and drafting for all styles of coats. III. Title.
GT610.S47   1994
391'.1'097309034--dc20
                                           94-37721
                                              CIP

Dedication

This work is dedicated to
Betty Williams
who knows more than almost
anyone about historical men's
fashions and tailoring. Her
generosity and support has
always been unconditional.
Without her it would not
have happened.

Contents

Introduction

The 1860s was an interesting period for the entire western world, and events always find their way into fashion, some of it short term and some of it very long term.

American fashions for both men and women were determined by the fashions of Paris and London. London especially with its well defined tailoring industry and men's fashion magazines was looked to by the tailors of the United States for fashion guidance. However, it must be pointed out that for the most part the fashion plates used in the English magazines in the early 1860s actually came from Paris. The pattern drafts were English.

Some of the more outstanding events in Europe just prior to and during this time were the Crimean War in which England and France were allied with Turkey against Russia. This increased the influence of Turkey, the 'mysterious East', and the muslim worlds in the fashions of Europe and then the United States, For instance smoking caps in the shape of a fez and the use of rich oriental fabrics in dressing gowns. Italy became unified and Garibaldi was the hero of the day, which led to Garibaldi jackets and shirts being worn by women and children, and Garbaldi suits for boys. Napoleon III was emperor in France and his court set the standards for French fashion. The French presence in Algeria brought us the Zouave uniforms and the Zouave fashions for women and boys.

In the United States the period is dominated by the Civil War in most people's minds, but it must also be remembered that it is also the time of the attempted impeachment of President Andrew Johnson, and the period known as the Reconstruction, which was nothing to be proud of and left a lot of resentment.

But most of all the 1860s was a period of mourning for both England and the United States. England because Prince Albert died in 1861 and Queen Victoria never really did come out of mourning for the event. The United States because it had lost well over 600,000 men in the Civil War and that left great imbalance and hardship in the nation.

However it must be pointed out that when people say: 'Men's fashions didn't change during the entire Victorian Era', or 'The only color worn was black', or 'Men only wore frock coats', then the answer is that they are not looking closely enough. Not only that, there also is a great difference between a fashion plate and what is worn on the street (or the battlefield). Just as there is usually a vast difference between a posed 'formal' portrait and a candid shot, not only in content but in the clothes that were worn. Newspaper engravings were widespread during this period and they too throw a different light on what people were actually wearing. Added to this there is the influence of geographical location, class, and the financial standing of the various people on what they wore.

As we will see, the 1860s was a period of transition and as such has a large variety of men's clothing both civilian and military.

MISSING.

He comes not; we have watched the green leaves springing
  Upon the maple-trees, beneath whose shade,
Glad as the blue-bird in its branches singing,
  Our soldier brother in his childhood played.

He comes not yet; though, while those boughs were leafless,
  Peace o'er our bleeding land her mantle flung;
And now November tears the crimson banner,
  October on the maple-trees had hung.

He comes not, yet we seem about to meet him,
  If we but hear the murmur of the breeze;
And, oh! how many times we've sprung to greet him,
  When leaves have rustled on the maple-trees.

He comes not; how 'twould ease this ceaseless aching
  If he but slept with kindred 'neath the hill;
They rest in peace, but our sad hearts are breaking
  Because of him—for he is missing still.   M. B.

Peterson's Magazine 1866

Acknowledgements
I especially wish to thank the following for their help with this project:
Janet Burgess, *Amazon Drygoods*
Robert Kaufmann, *Costume Institute Library, Metropolitan Museum of Art*
Mike McAfee, *West Point Museum*
Kevin Seligman, *Northern Illinois University*
Fred Struthers
Margaret Vining, *Smithsonian Institution*
Betty Williams, *Studio - NYC*

Civilian Men's Wear

Notes on Civilian Men's Wear

The 1860s is a very interesting period for men's wear. It is a transitional period between the frock coat and the more formal men's wear of the early 1850s, and the beginnings of the 'lounge suit' that we now think of as a businessman's suit. The result is that there is a great range of clothes for men.

As previously noted, American tailors looked mostly to the English for guidance both in tailoring matters and in fashion. However, of the major fashion magazines Minister's <u>Gazette of Fashion</u> definitely got its fashion plates from Paris, and Devere who published the <u>Gentlemen's Magazine</u> always maintained a French connection. But Giles in his *Art of Cutting & History of English Costume* does not venture to say where Devere's plates were coming from. The illustrations in the <u>Tailor & Cutter</u>, which started about 1866 are more reliably English.

At the same time, the American tailoring industry (especially in New York) was making great strides on its own. It is interesting to see an "American Frock Coat" appear in an issue of the <u>Tailor & Cutter</u>. They say that it appeared first in <u>The Cutter Monthly</u>, which had to have been an American publication. We reproduce this pattern here along with the editor's comments. Please take into account that this is for experienced tailors. For those who are not familiar with the term, a <u>*scye*</u> is a tailoring term for the curved lower segment of the arm-hole of a coat.

The (following) diagrams are those of a frock coat, copied from "The Cutter Monthly," by Mr. W. Glencross, New York. A specimen of this author's trouser system was inserted in this journal a few weeks since. We learn from several quarters that the system is giving satisfaction to those of our subscribers who have tried it, and we have no doubt but the frock coat pattern, when carefully made up, will give similar results. The size of the model is eighteen breast and sixteen waist, and intended to fit a well-made customer, and such a one as can carry a broad shoulder, and bear his coat fit close about the scye. This later peculiarity is a source of great annoyance to most cutters, and constitutes one of the principle difficulties in coat cutting; ease and close-fitting are almost irreconcilable, the one often proving antagonistic to the attainment of the other. Customers are often very fidgety about being touched in front of scye, and must have ease at that part, come from where it may, and the beauty and symmetry of many a well cut coat have been nullified, through advancing the scye beyond a point absolutely required by the form or size of the figure. We are under the impression that not many Britishers will be found to wear a coat cut exactly in the American style. The pattern can be produced for a larger or a smaller size, by

American Frock Coat.

BY WILLIAM GLENCROSS.

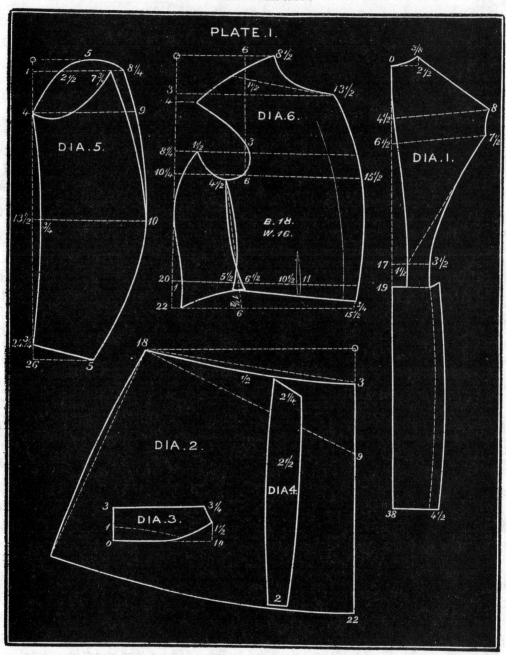

Tailor and Cutter 1869

using the graduated tapes; and in anticipation of having to enlarge the arm-hole, we would advise the shoulder being made a little straighter, so as to retain the same shape of scye, and to bear in mind that if a change is contemplated to be made in the scye, to make a corresponding alteration in the sleeve top, otherwise it will be found too small. We may state, for the satisfaction of our readers, that Mr. Glencross is an enthusiastic propounder of measurement system, and that his plan of taking the measures is somewhat different to that in general use, more particularly his method of taking the diameter of the arm; for this purpose he employs two straight-edges or rulers - the one he places below the arm, the other on the shoulder, the edges being kept parallel - while this placed he measures the space between them for depth of scye. Then he will reverse the position of the rulers, placing one in front, the other at the back of the arm, in a perpendicular position, and the space between them indicate the size of the arm in a lateral direction. By the result of these ascertained quantities, the size and form of the arm-hole is regulated. Our experimenting friends can try this process, and we have no doubt they will be able to take an idea out of the principle and apply it with advantage, without following the *routine* laid down in the original system. - Ed. Cutter.

There was not a lot of rapid movement in fashions in the 1860s but there seems to be a trend towards a more relaxed look as the decade moves along. This will lead to the 'sack suit' or 'lounge suit' of the late '60s and 1870s. Vests were very decorative, as were suspenders and braces (see the *Accessories* section for instructions on how to make braces). Trousers often were of highly patterned material - sometimes matching the vest, most often not. In a very few instances one can even see a '3 piece suit' of matching material in the fashion plates.

Informal, indoor clothing often exhibited more of a flair and had an oriental or Turkish flavor, both in shape and the use of materials. This is especially true of dressing gowns, smoking caps, slippers, and shawls. One of the 1863 fashion plates shows a dressing gown. A pattern for this type dressing gown can be found in Devere's *The Handbook of Practical Cutting on the Centre Point System*, plate 22, page 102, using figure 3 for the sleeve. Fashion plates do not show men wearing shawls, but it is known that they were worn. There was no central heating and the houses were cold and drafty in the winters. Shawls were also used in carriages by both men and women. It is said that Lincoln had a preference for Paisley shawls which were both popular and plentiful in the 1860s. Instructions (but no illustration) for a Gentlemen's Comforter can be found in Hartley's *The Ladies Hand Book of Fancy & Ornamental Work*.

Cravats, or ties, were very narrow and tied in a flat bow or knotted. A pattern for this type cravat appears in the *Accessories* section.

One of the most widespread capes used during this period for outdoors and travel was the Inverness cape, a pattern and instructions for an Inverness will follow this discussion. It comes from the Tailor & Cutter

1869. The frock overcoat (a surtout, or top coat), a paletot which was loosely cut, and the Chesterfield which was cut like a sack coat only looser (also called a paletot-sac, or driving coat, or oversack), were all worn as overcoats.

A number of hats were worn, the most universal being the top hat, usually made of silk. In the mid-1860s the crown was lowered to about six inches. Other hats of the period were the bowler, straight brimmed straw hats in summer, cloth caps for sport, and particularly in America there appear to be a lot of soft felt hats.

Short boots and button boots were common in the 1860s and the late 1860s saw the advent of front laced boots. Laced shoes and buttoned shoes were also worn. Both boots and shoes became a bit wider and the toe rounded a little in this period. Gaiters were worn in the country. A pattern for gaiters appears in the *Accessories* section.

Civil War Era Etiquette has a section of 'Dress' in it, and one of the things it says is: " A well-dressed man does not require so much an extensive as a varied wardrobe.. He wants a different costume for every season and every occasion; but if what he selects is simple rather than striking, he may appear in the same clothes as often as he likes, as long as they are fresh and appropriate to the season and the object. There are four kinds of coats which he must have: a business coat, a frock-coat, a dress-coat, and an over-coat. A well dressed man may do well with four of the first, and one of each of the others per annum. An economical man can get along with less.". The book has a lot of good advice for both men and women on dress and many other subjects.

For another look at what was being worn in this period, note the baseball players in the 1865 section of *Additional Illustrations*.

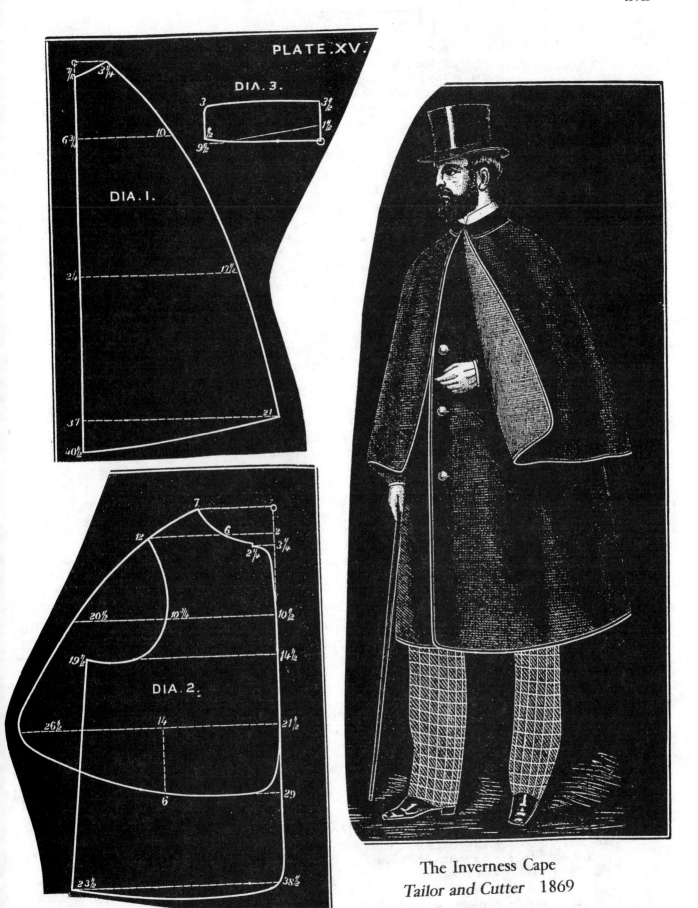

The Inverness Cape
Tailor and Cutter 1869

THE INVERNESS CAPE,

Diagrams 1, 2, and 3, Plate 15,

Is a style of garment always more or less in demand. particularly for travelling, and is also a favourite with many gentlemen as a kind of throw over all when returning from evening parties, theatre, and places of recreation; the ease with which they can be put on or taken off, and the quantity of drapery in them, admitting of being wrapped round the body, adding warmth, and at the same time tending to make their impress on the feelings of the wearer still greater.

The amount of fulness or drapery put in this style of over-coat depend in a great measure on taste; but, like all other loose-hanging garments, anything like contraction at any part detract very materially from their graceful aspect. When forming this particular style of coat, there is one point requiring special attention; we refer to the width given to the fore-part at $19\frac{1}{2}$, if too narrow at this part, no matter what width is given to the back, the shoulder seam being too forward, press against the back of the arm, and cause the coat to feel as if too narrow across the chest. The diagrams represent a cape of a medium degree of fulness, the length is adjusted for a person about 5 feet 7 inches, and measuring 36 to 37 on the vest; the length is to the short side, but can be easily extended, as may be desired; they are generally worn very long—about mid-way between the calf of the leg and ankle is a good criterion for length—not too long for walking, and keep the knees and legs well protected in a storm.

Our diagrams are arranged to be drawn out to the full size by the inch tape, the quantities on them representing inches, and not units of any scale of size.

The Back, Diagram 1,

Is drawn out by marking down $\frac{7}{8}$, $6\frac{3}{4}$, 24, 37, $40\frac{1}{2}$, the widths being $3\frac{1}{4}$, 10, $17\frac{1}{2}$, 21. If required less ample, contract it at $17\frac{1}{2}$ and 21; the width at 10 must not be reduced, except the shoulders are low and small; and if high and large, add more round at 10.

The Fore-part. Diagram 2.

The depth points are 2, $3\frac{1}{4}$, $10\frac{1}{2}$, $14\frac{1}{2}$, $21\frac{1}{2}$, 29, $38\frac{1}{2}$; square across and mark 7, 6, 12, $2\frac{1}{4}$, $10\frac{3}{4}$, $20\frac{1}{2}$, $19\frac{1}{2}$, 14, 6 down, $26\frac{1}{2}$, $23\frac{1}{2}$. The wing and fore-part are formed at the same time—this is not imperative, and they may be drafted separately; in all cases the wing must be of the exact same shape as the fore-part, up the front, neck, and shoulder, as far as the front 12; if wanted with more fulness, add to the quantities $20\frac{1}{2}$ and $26\frac{1}{2}$. The front is intended to be single-breasted, either with or without a fly; the buttons are to stand about three inches from the edge.

The Collar, Diagram 3,

Must be cut nearly straight on the sewing-on edge, and if to be continually worn buttoned up, or of the Prussian style, the sewing-on edge must be cut hollow, and pressed out to the form of a cape, round on both edges. There is no established rule in which the fronts are made up and collar put on; occasionally the front of the wing is made up the same with three or four holes and buttons; some houses fasten the wing to the neck right to the front step, others separate them from the hollow of neck, and sew the collar to either wing or fore-part—generally to the latter when the front is intended to turn down, and to the wing when made always to button up.

The Inverness can be drawn out to any size by using the graduated tapes; for sizes below 18 breast, take a scale one inch of a side larger than the size in the vest, and half an inch of a side for the larger sizes. These coats are seldom lined throughout, except for special purpose; when made from thin material, and required warm, they may be lined to a level with the bottom of the arm-hole; when this is done, the wing must also be lined. The pockets are generally laid on and made large, with flaps to cover the top. Heather mixture and grey Tweed are the materials mostly used for this style of garment.

Tailor and Cutter 1869

Salisbury's System

Notes on Salisbury's System
including Names of Garments

There are few if any other American tailoring systems, as opposed to individual pattern drafts, that have survived from this period. There are English systems like Devere's *The Handbook of Practical Cutting on the Centre Point System*, which is very useful for making garments of the 1860s (especially specialty garments that are not in the Salisbury system, such as riding habits, hunting clothes, dressing gowns, etc.), but it is not American and in dealing with the Civil War period it seems fitting to take advantage of the American system that is available.

Salisbury (Wilbur S.) copyrighted this work in 1865, the date on the copyright page was altered to this in ink and that is also what the records show. He was, at that time, in New York where most of the tailoring industry was centered. Also in 1865 he wrote *Salisbury's System and Tables of Combined Measure...* Watertown, NY. It is hard to know what that might have been and how it differs from the present work as this too has a table of combined measures.

The next work was five years later when he published *Salisbury's Revised Work on Coat Cutting...*published in Battle Creek, Michigan in 1870. He also edited a magazine The Tailor's Intelligence: an Illustrated Monthly Magazine Devoted to the Art & Science of Garment Cutting... Volume I, August 1870.

It seems strange that he moved from New York which was the center of the American tailoring world to Battle Creek, Michigan which was very small and fairly remote. It was only incorporated as a city in 1859.

The only other work that shows up in the copyright records is *Salisbury's Great Pantaloons System, devoted to the Aesthetics of Pantaloon Cutting, etc.* by W.S. and B. Salisbury; Battle Creek, Michigan by the "Review and herald steam book and job printing house".

Please note that the Salisbury system has been printed in its original form, including blank pages. The only exception being that all the drafts have been identified with the names of the garments for greater clarity. **Also note that although the title indicates that the book only covers coats, it also has vests and trousers, making it a complete system of tailoring.**

Names of Garments

Frock coat - always had a waist seam and a separate skirt, except for the center back pieces. The center front of the shirts came down straight and had square corners at the bottom. Most of the time the lapel and center front of the body is a separate piece. A frock coat can be single breasted (S.B.) or double breasted (D.B.).

Cutaway Frock - Also known as a cutaway coat or a morning coat. This is exactly like the frock coat except that it is always single breasted, the lapel is not a separate piece and the center front of the skirts are cut away at an angle and have rounded corners at the bottom. This is what Salisbury calls a **'New York Walking Coat'**.

Sack coat - Also known as a body sack coat, or a sac or lounge coat. This has no waist seam and at this period no side back piece. There is very little shaping and is shorter than the frock or the cutaway. It can be single breasted or double breasted. This is what Salisbury calls a **'French Walking Coat'**.

Paletot - Also known as a body paletot, or Oxanian or Tweedside (and just to be confusing some magazines also refer to this as a morning coat or a lounge coat!). At this period it is very much like a frock coat except that there is no waist seam on the front piece. There is always a side back piece with a waist seam, and the lapel is always part of the front piece. This is what Salisbury calls an **'English Walking Coat'**.

Dress coat - This always has tails. Aside from the fact that the skirt is cut into tails it is exactly like a frock coat including the separate lapel piece.

Surtout - Also known as a frock overcoat or top coat. This is cut exactly like a frock coat except that it is bigger and longer.

Paletot (overcoat) -Also known as a half-sack overcoat. This is exactly like a paletot except that it is cut looser and longer.

Chesterfield - Also known as a paletot-sac, or driving coat, or oversack. This is a overcoat cut like a sack coat except that it is looser and longer.

New York Walking Coat
(cutaway frock)

SALISBURY'S

System of Actual

Measurement and Drafting,

FOR ALL STYLES OF COATS,

UPON

GEOMETRICAL PRINCIPLES.

BY

W. S. SALISBURY,

DESIGNER, PATTERN CUTTER,

—AND—

TEACHER OF GARMENT CUTTING.

1866.

F. SOMERS, PRINTER AND STEREOTYPER,
211 Centre Street, N. Y.

CONTENTS.

"ERRATA."

Under the heading To Measure, on Plate I, in parenthesis, should read thus, (Fig. 1 & 3.)

ON PLATE VIII,

where it says from $11\frac{1}{4}$ sweep 15, should read from $11\frac{1}{4}$ sweep $12\frac{3}{4}$.

ON PLATE IX,

to draft fore part, should take the place of to draft the sleeve, and *vice versa.*

ON PLATE X,

where it reads, represents a Boy's Paletot Coat, should read Body Paletot Coat.

PREFACE.

IN presenting this work, I have the *assurance* of meeting the wants of the trade, by furnishing a system of actual measurement, combining pure geometrical principles with simplicity, in drafting all styles of *over* and *under-coats*, with the use of *tape-measure* and square, only; it is a system of measuring and drafting that will reach every shape, thereby giving us the high or low shoulder, erect or stooping form, shoulder, back or forwards, narrow or wide arm-scye, narrow or wide back-strop; in fact, producing a correct draft for all forms in as simple a manner as possible.

The illustration I give of a metallic square for measuring, has been in use to a considerable extent; nevertheless it is entirely new to the majority of cutters. I can say, without fear of contradiction, that it is all any cutter may require, to gain access to the most important points, and to establish reliable measurement of the uneven surface of the *human body*. Any person receiving this work should give the above their undivided attention, until they are conversant with its utility in measuring. You may raise objections against its simplicity, for the very reason that you have been confined to some complicated *instrument* or *harness* to measure from, and acquired a considerable notoriety as a custom cutter, after years of close attentive study and practice, and such a reason alone is sufficient to arrest your attention to this subject.

To bring forward a few seeming objections, without an investigation, candidly considered, is leaving that which is certain, to launch off into the field of uncertainty. It is leaving the path of truth and light, to leap into the dark, and grope in darkness.

As well might we deny the benefits of the sun, and try to withdraw ourselves from its genial rays, because it has been ascertained that it has spots which do not emit light.

Who knows but that these points which are not clear for the time being, will, when understood, elucidate the truth, and prove to be some of the strongest arguments in our favor? It is not prudent to be always looking at objections. We are living in a time and age, when *minds* with the experience of generations are upon the eve of the most wonderful and astonishing discoveries of modern invention: it is universally conceded that the first improvements are generally too complicated for practical use. Time and experience justify the claims, and improvements in all branches of industry have been rapid. It is only about fifteen years since invention took its *aerial* flight in our country, and every branch of science owes its allegiance to the inventor; the tide is changing, and minds that have wrought by experience, say, simplicity is needed to ensure success to inventors.

For a number of years, in cutting custom work, I have confined myself exclusively to making a pattern for nearly every *coat*, (that is the body part only), and in this way, (see Plate 8), I would cut the *back* and forepart out of paper, then finish the balance of my coat on cloth. I found in this way the various shape of shoulders and their changes, and by using different instruments of my own and other inventors, I have had partial success in keeping my coats properly balanced. I can assure you that we may use all the various improvements in measuring, and establish the points necessary, and accurately, yet all may be lost in drafting, by not understanding the relations of the various points to the balance of the *body*, thereby having a coat too low in the neck, or too high ; the neck gorge too long, front too full, too tight under the arm, or the back may hang off at waist, with many other grievances that finally become fixed facts, and are palmed off on your customer with some excuse about careless workmen, when you alone are to blame. Now if I can in any way be a benefit to the trade, in a moral or practical point, it will give me a deal of satisfaction.

The back never should be drafted parallel with line A, Plate 1, but by line B, unless the back is to be cut without seam in the middle. If you do, you lose the relative positions existing between the *bust* and *curve* measures, and the *curve measure* could not be applied directly. It will be observed in measuring, I establish beyond a doubt the two points (and only two) necessary to establish the third (or shoulder point) by, in drafting. It will also be observed I make line A the principal, or balance line, in diagram 2, (as in all drafts).

Let the person receiving this work, make a full draft of the different diagrams, and study the various changes, caused by malformation in the *human body.*

PLATES 5 and 6 present two extremes, although the *breast measures* are the same, and will, upon investigation of their changes in relation to each other, show all that is required as an explanation to an *extra erect* form or a stooping structure.

NOTE.—The shoulder point is attained by three measures in their relations to the two points established by the instrument, and the measure from 0 at neck, to 3 on back seam, also the various positions of different lines running perpendicular and horizontally to the body, when drafting, to *illustrate.*—If we should call the measure 9, on Plate 5, $9\frac{1}{3}$, you would see readily that it would make the coat too high in neck, (providing the first measure 9 was correctly taken), it would also throw shoulder point forward, and cause a depression at neck of coat, too tight at back waist, and loose across the shoulder. If we make measure 15 too long, our coat will hang off at bottom of waist, if too short, it will depress at neck, full on back of shoulder, and under the arm. If we get measure $19\frac{1}{2}$, too long, over the shoulder, it will carry the shoulder point off from the neck, and full across the shoulders, if too short, will carry shoulder point forward and cut under the arm, and if we take the measure from front of scye to center of back, $12\frac{1}{2}$, too long, it will give loose cloth across the shoulder blades ; if too short, will cut front of shoulders. Now let these measures be taken with care, and we have a well balanced coat around the shoulders.

NOTE.—If we apply our gorge measure correctly, we shall be able to overcome a great difficulty, with most of workmen, that is, a surplus amount of cloth at breast, or too long gorge. This measure should always be taken.

PLATE 6 we have what constitutes a stooping structure, in the lengthening of measure from neck joint to 3 ($9\frac{7}{8}$), and shortening measure front of scye to neck joint, ($13\frac{1}{2}$), also over the shoulder, $19\frac{1}{4}$, and in lengthening of measure from front of scye to centre of back, $13\frac{1}{2}$, and giving more width to back strop, we find the *stooping form*, whereas we found an erect structure in diagram 5. By making a full draft from these diagrams, you will become perfectly conversant with the different shapes. Some will observe : How can a wider back be used than is established in measuring, without making the arm-scye too narrow, thereby deranging the whole draft. I will say, you may make just as wide a back as the style demands, by applying the exact width of back strop, as taken from line **A** diagram 2, out across the top part of the side body on line B, the remainder of measure $11\frac{1}{4}$, with an additional $\frac{1}{2}$ inch forward on line B, to give width to scye. You will thereby preserve an equal balance to the different points.

Plate 1.

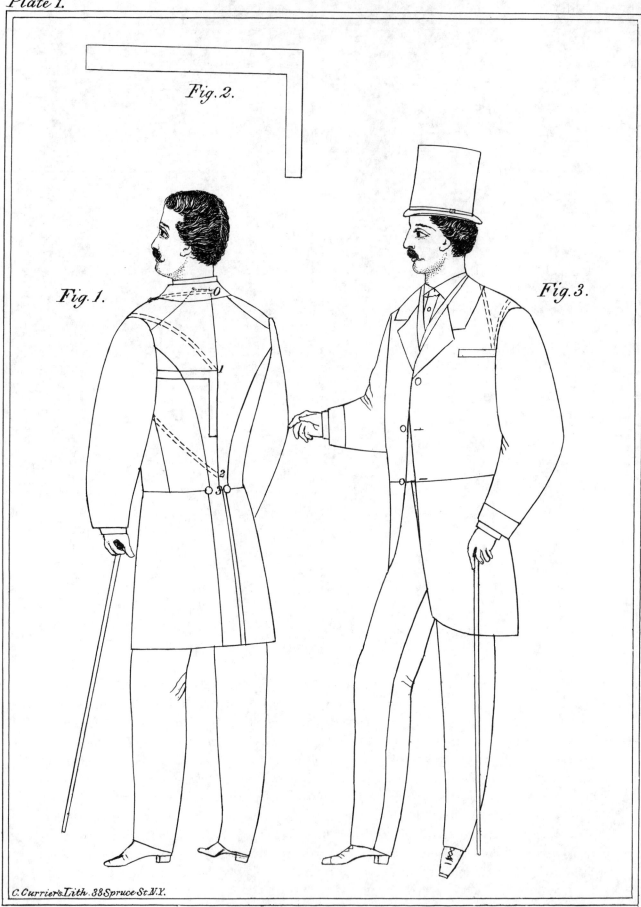

Fig. 2.

Fig. 1.

Fig. 3.

New York Walking Coat
(cutaway frock)

PLATE I.

WE have on this Plate three figures illustrated. The first and second represent the way to take the Four Proof Measures, with the instrument (Fig. 2), shown as applied when establishing the two points, namely, centre of back in line with front of scye. First, in preparatory to measuring you want a good fitting coat on your customer to take the measure over, with the following qualifications as near as possible : let the coat envelope the body smoothly, not too high up under the arm, or not too low, (in either case you would be liable to the same fault in your work), and have the coat buttoned.

THE INSTRUMENT

Should be made of heavy sheet tin or other suitable material, perfectly square, fourteen inches in length, by one and one half inches wide (for the long arm), and eight inches long, by one wide (for the short arm). See Cut Fig. 2. Then bend the long arm, so it will conform to the shape of the body.

TO MEASURE:

Mark point O, Fig. 1, at the neck-joint, under the collar. Then take the instrument, place it under the arm, (see Figs. 2 & 3) close, so it will not crowd or cause your customer to raise his shoulder, then bring the short arm in line with center of back seam, as seen in Fig. 1. Then chalk-mark top side of instrument at point 1, on the back seam; also front of the shoulder along the top side of instrument. Then place the wooden square against the front of shoulder, parallel with the body, and mark down across chalk-mark, remove square and instrument, and we have two important points established. Now take the wooden square and slip the long arm under the arm of your customer from the back side, and where the short arm of the square crosses the back-scye, make a chalk-mark for width of natural back; be sure and have the long arm lay up close to the body, while the short arm stands perpendicular. Make a mark at 2, the hollow or natural waist, at 3 for the length of waist; which is governed by style. Having all the important points located, place the tape-measure at O, measure to 1, 8½, to 2, 17¼, (see Plate 2) also to 19½, then 38 full length of coat; now start from front of scye at the point marked, and measure over shoulder to O, at the neck-joint, 12¾, from the same point to 1 on the back seam 16¾, then out to 1 on the back 11¼, then down to 2, the eleptic 12½. Said measures should be taken close, now around the arm-scye 17, then raise the right arm of your customer and bend the elbow so it will be at right angles with the body, then commence and measure from the center of back-seam to mark made for natural width of back 7, then to the elbow-joint 19½, then to the knuckle-joint of the little finger 32 inches. Now the neck gorge measure from O, passing under the collar to the center of neck in front, 8½. Lastly the breast, 38, which should be taken with care, by passing the hands across the shoulder-blades, bringing the measure close up under the arm-pits, *over the vest*, forward on breast; let the customer stand erect and natural; the waist-measure, 32, to be taken in the smallest part of the body; the hip-measure, 35, over the hip-bone, at the top.

Plate 2.

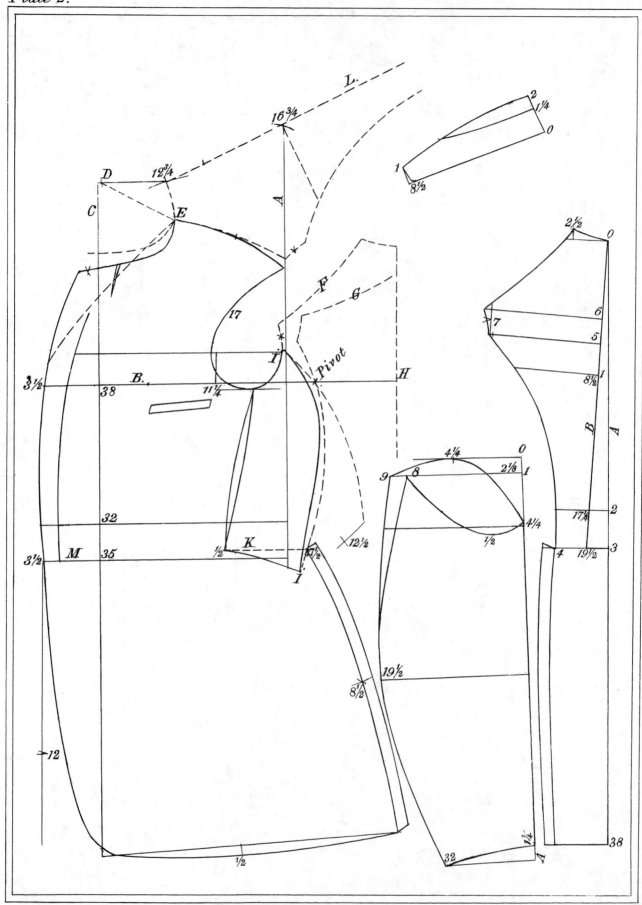

Paletot (body paletot)

PLATE II.

TO DRAFT.

WE will commence with the back on Plate 2.

Draw line *A*,

From *O*, square out with line A, 2½ inches, or ⅛ of 19, one-half the breast.

From *O*, measure to 2, 17¼, to 3, 19½, then to 38 ; square out at 2, 3 and 38.

From 3, go in to 19½, 1½ inches, always for a Dress or Frock Coat ; then draw line *B* to *O*.

From 19½ to 4, 2 inches, or the style ; then ¾ to 1 inch for fold, as shown by the two lines.

From *O*, measure down on line *B* 8½, then up to 5; ⅛ of 19, or one-half of breast ; to 6 1½ or 2 inches as the style may govern.

Square out with line *B*, from 8½, 5 and 6.

From 5, give width to natural back 7, draw line and add ¼ inch, or as much more as required for style, or full width of the back strop.

TO DRAFT FOREPART.

Draw line *A*, and place the back in keeping with same, and mark at 8½, 17¼ and 19½, on line *A ;* then square out with line *A*.

Place the back as shown by dotted lines **F** ; then mark at *Pivot*, remembering to have the natural width of the back in keeping with line *A*, (as shown more fully on Plate 3), and then all the extra width added to the natural back is forward of line *A*.

From *H*, measure in on line B, 11¼ inches, adding ½ inch, which would make 11¾ ; then to 38, 19½ inches, which gives the center of the breast ; then square line *C* by line *B*.

From 11¼ sweep 12½, adding ½ of an inch, which would be 13 inches ; then swing in the bottom of back by the pivot until 17¼ intersects with sweep 12½, as shown by dotted lines *G*.

Form curve to side body, as shown ; let the curve to side body be the same length as the curve to the back, measuring from *I* to *I*, on a straight line ; form the width of side body according to style.

From 11¼, sweep 12¾, adding ½ inch.

From 11¼, sweep 16¾ inches across line *A*.

Now place the back, as shown by dotted lines *L*, having 8½ on the back placed at 16¾ on line *A*, the top of the back intersecting sweep 12¾, which gives the true pitch of shoulder, establishing the shoulder-point accurately in all cases.

Form the curve to shoulder, giving the same length, as the curve to the top of back.

Form the scye as shown.

From *D*, square out to sweep 12¾, with line *C*.

From D to E is $\frac{1}{4}$ of 19, one-half of the breast. Place the thumb at D, sweep from E until it crosses line C. Form the gorge to style.

From 38, go out on line B, $3\frac{1}{2}$ inches, to form the edge of coat; also from 35, on line M.

From $3\frac{1}{2}$ line M, square down 12 inches, or two-thirds of 18, one-half of the hip.

From $17\frac{1}{2}$ sweep $8\frac{1}{2}$ inches; then from 12, sweep from $17\frac{1}{2}$ until it crosses sweep at $8\frac{1}{2}$, which gives the point for curve to the skirt, which finish to the length of back.

From $\frac{1}{2}$ draw dotted line K, the length of the bottom of side body from $\frac{1}{2}$ to I.

THE SLEEVE.

To draft, draw line from O to A.

From O measure down 1 inch; then $4\frac{1}{4}$, or one-fourth of the scye measure, 17 inches.

Square out at O, $4\frac{1}{4}$, or $\frac{1}{4}$ of scye.

Square out at 1, $2\frac{1}{8}$, or one-eighth of scye measure.

From 1 to 9 is one-half of scye, and $\frac{1}{2}$ inch, making 9 inches; come in one inch for under side of the sleeve; take the width of the back, and apply at 9.

From 9, less the full width of back, to $19\frac{1}{2}$, the elbow measure; then to 32, the full length; form the curves to style.

THE COLLAR.

To draft the collar, draw lines as given.

From O, $8\frac{1}{2}$ inches, $1\frac{1}{4}$, and 2 inches.

From $8\frac{1}{2}$, one inch.

TO RECAPITULATE.

The measures taken stand thus:

$8\frac{1}{2}$, $17\frac{1}{4}$, $19\frac{1}{2}$, 38.

$12\frac{3}{4}$, $16\frac{3}{4}$, $11\frac{1}{4}$, $12\frac{1}{2}$.

Scye, 17, 7, $19\frac{1}{2}$, 32.

Gorge, 9, 38, 32. Hip 35.

As was taken from a young man, 5 feet 8 inches high, erect, full round bust.

The draft is for a Body Paletot, to be drawn as represented.

Plate 3.

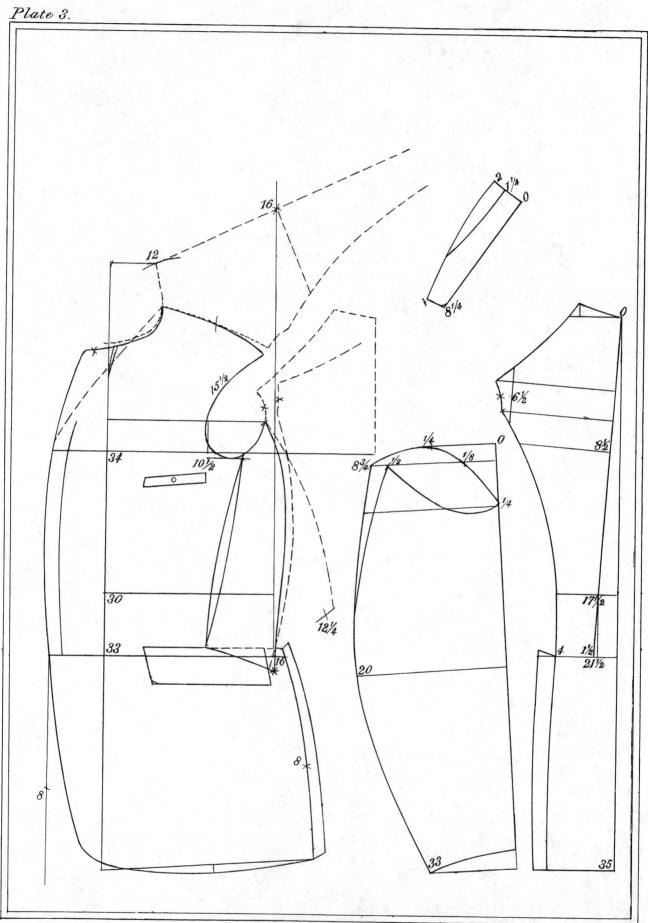

English Walking Coat
(single breasted paletot)

PLATE III.

WE have on this Plate the diagrams for a single-breasted English Walking Coat. Long in the waist, with medium-length Skirt, to be drafted as given. The measure was taken from a young man 5 feet 9 inches high, tall and slender, flat shoulder blades, very hollow back, and long-waisted, which we give as the *Tall and Slender form.*

The measures stand thus :

$8\frac{1}{2}$, $17\frac{1}{2}$, $21\frac{1}{2}$, 35,

12, 16, $10\frac{1}{2}$, $12\frac{1}{4}$,

Scye, $15\frac{1}{2}$, $6\frac{1}{2}$, 20, 33,

Gorge, 8, 34, 30. Hip, 33.

Form draft to Diagrams. The Figures give the measure as taken.

Plate 4.

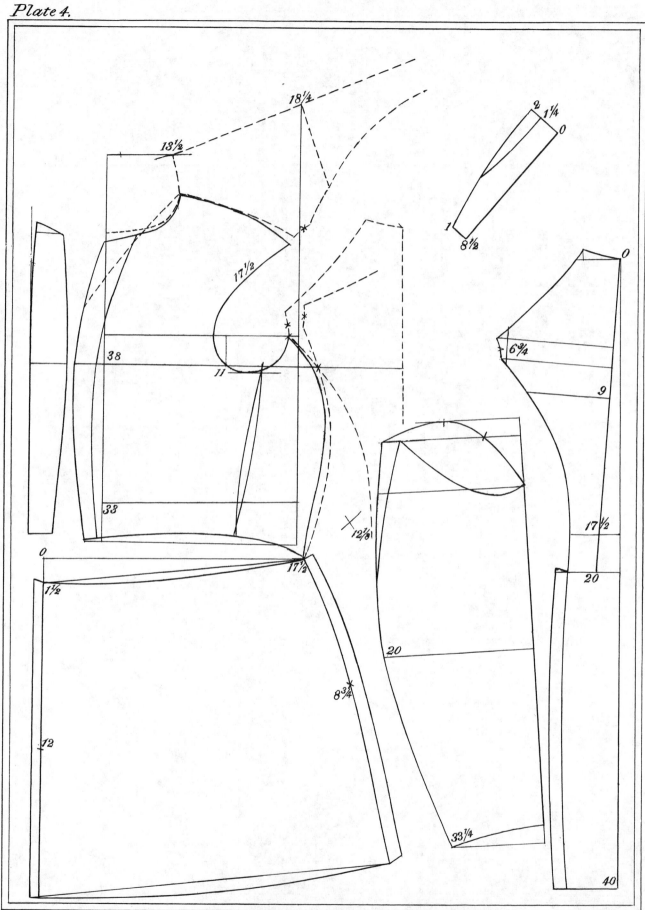

Double-Breasted Frock-coat

PLATE IV.

WE have on this Plate the diagrams for a Double-Breasted Frock-Coat, with Lapel cut off; drawn to the measure taken from a young man, Tall, Erect, High Shoulders and Narrow Back Strop, with a full bust, standing 5 feet 10 inches high, which I give as the *Tall Erect Form*.

The measures stand thus:

9, 17½, 20, 40.

13½, 18¼, 11, 12⅛.

Scye, 17½, 6¾, 20, 33¼.

Gorge, 8½, 38, 33. Hip, 35.

Draft according to the Diagrams, letting the style govern the widths and lengths.

Plate 5.

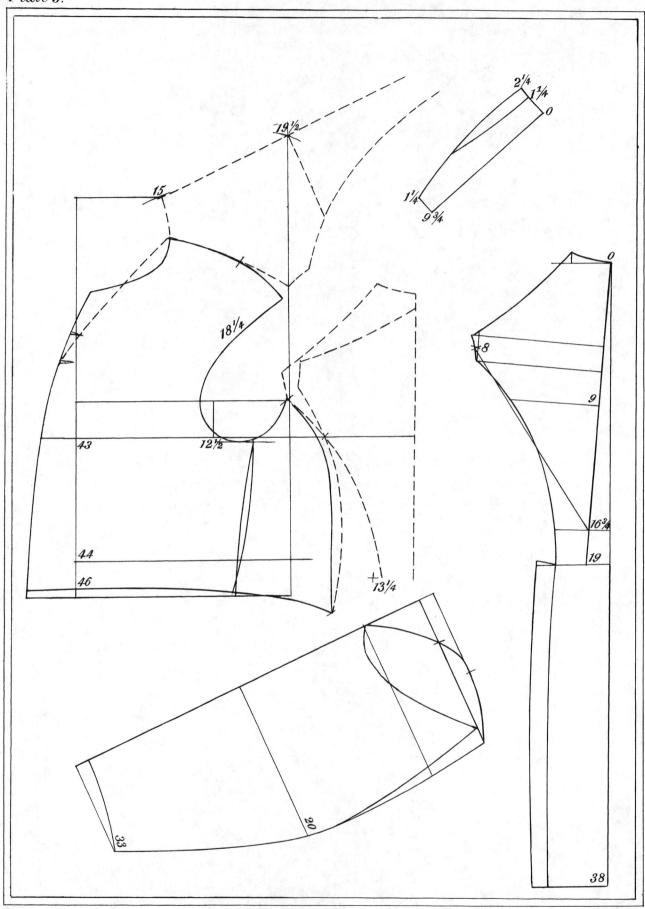

Double-Breasted Frock-coat
(stout person)

PLATE V.

WE have represented on this Plate the Diagrams for the Stout or Corpulent built person. The draft is for a Double-Breasted Frock—with the Skirt on Plate 6.—We then have the draft complete. Taken from a man 5 feet 9 inches high, Erect, Flat across the shoulder-blades, Short Neck, Short Waist, and Corpulent.

The measures stand thus:

9, 16¾, 19, 38.

15, 19½, 12½, 13¼.

Scye, 18¼, 8, 21, 33.

Gorge, 9¾, 43, 44. Hip, 46, or around the largest part of the Waist. This draft shows in itself the form of the man, Shoulder thrown back, and the Waist forward, as does every draft, when made properly. They bring out the shape of the person measured correctly.

Plate 6.

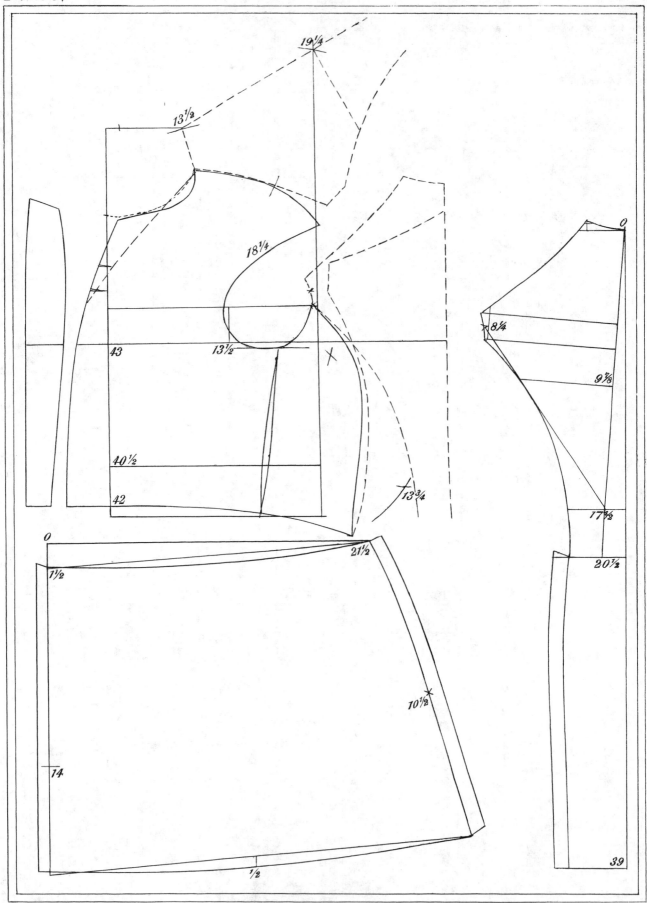

Double-Breasted Frock-coat
(stooping person)

PLATE VI.

WE have represented on this Plate the Diagrams for a Double-Breasted Frock—with the sleeve and collar on Plate 5.

The draft is for the *Extreme Stooping* person and shows its characteristics. The same as the diagram on Plate 5, in the Shoulder being forward, the Waist thrown in. The draft was taken from a man 5 feet 8 inches high, Stoop Shoulder, Neck thrown Forward, Wide Back Strop.

The measures stand thus:

$9\frac{7}{8}$, $17\frac{1}{2}$, $20\frac{1}{2}$, 39.

$13\frac{1}{2}$, $19\frac{1}{4}$, $13\frac{1}{2}$, $13\frac{3}{4}$.

Scye, $18\frac{1}{4}$, $8\frac{1}{4}$, $21\frac{1}{2}$, $34\frac{3}{4}$.

Gorge, $9\frac{1}{4}$, 43, $40\frac{1}{2}$, 42.

Form draft to Diagrams. The Figures give the measure as taken.

Plate 7.

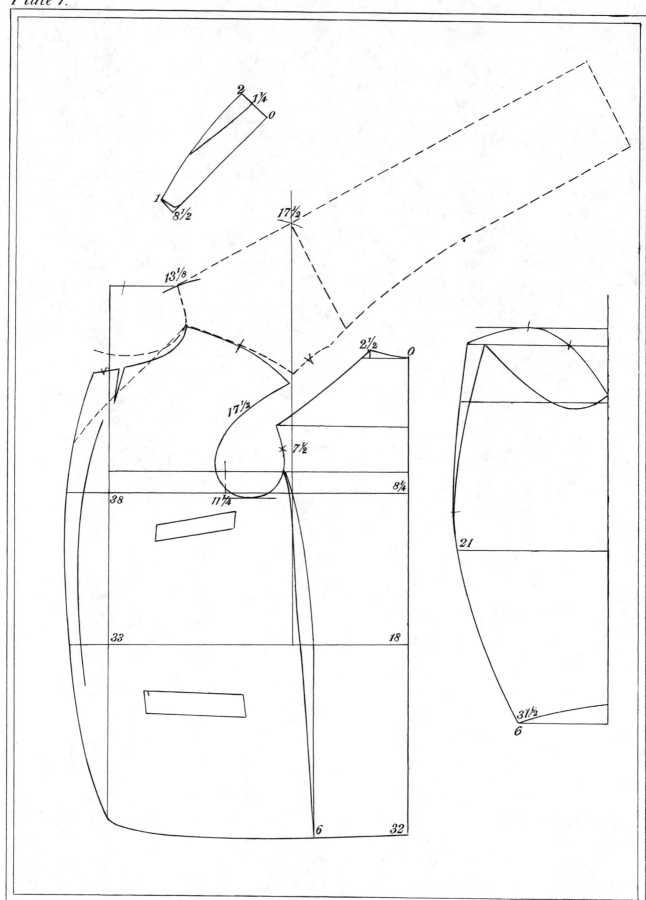

Body Sack Coat

PLATE VII.

THIS diagram represents the *Body Sack Coat*. Natural width of Back, 7½, full width 8½. This measure was taken from a young man, 5 feet 7 inches high.

The full measures are:

8¼, 18, 32.

13⅛, 17½, 11¼.

7½, 21, 31½.

Scye, 17½.

Gorge, 9, 38, 33.

The draft gives a complete idea in itself how to cut a Body Sack, or any kind of Sack, and how to properly balance the Coat.

Plate 8.

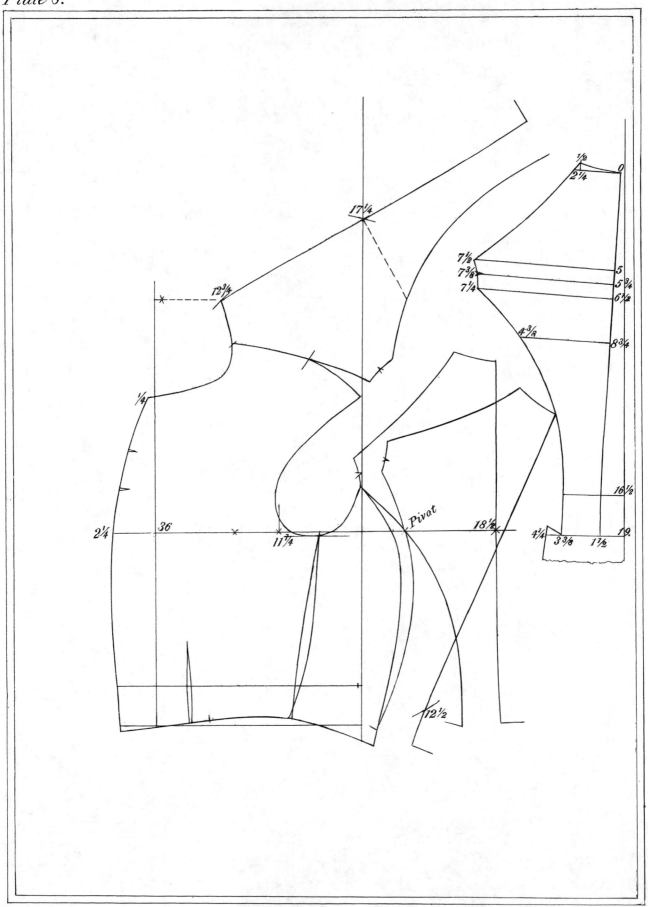

Model Draft
(for either frock or cutaway)

PLATE VIII.

REPRESENTS a model draft for size, thirty-six breast measure; also the uniform proof measures 8¾, 12¼, 17¼, 11¼, 12½, as used for getting up setts of Patterns. The distances are properly represented as taken in inches, from and to the different points on the body; it also shows all the draft from measure required for use. When cutting custom work, where from necessity one requires a model, cut from paper, so as to save time in laying out a coat on cloth, preparatory to cutting same; it also assists in a saving of cloth. The sleeve can be drafted on the cloth, or use a pattern; and the skirt and collar, the same way.

TO DRAFT THE BACK.

Draw line *A*, (Plate 2) from *O*, measure down 16½, then 19, (finishing the full length of skirt on the cloth.)

Square out from 16½ and 19.

Measure in from 19, one and one-half inches; and 3⅜; also 4¼, inches.

Draw line *B* from *O* to 1½.

From *O* measure down line *B*, 5, 5¾, 6½, 8¾ inches; then square out from line *B*.

From *O*, go out at top 2½; then up 1½ inch.

From 5, go out 7½ inches.

From 5¾, go out 7⅜ inches.

From 6½, go out 7¼ inches.

From 8¾, go out 4⅜ inches.

Finish by drawing curve lines.

TO DRAFT THE FOREPART.

Draw line *A*, (Plate 2) then lay the back thereto; marking on line *A*, corresponding with 8¾, 16½, 19, on the back, and square out with line *A*, extending the *balance* or breast line, *B*, as shown. Place the back in position, parallel with line *A*, and line *B*; lay off on line *B* 11¼ inches, adding ½ inch. (Said ½ inch being cut off in forming curve to side body at pivot.)

Measure from 11¼, and sweep 12½ inches; then swing the back in at pivot, until 16½ on the back intersects the sweep 12½.

Form curve to side body, as represented; the curve to side body should be about the same length as the curve to the back.

From 11¼, sweep 15, being the measure from front of scye, to the neck joint.

From 11¼, sweep 17¼, crossing line *A*; it being the measure from front of scye over the shoulder to 8¾, on the back; place 8¾ on the back at 17¼ on line *A*; the top of back touching sweep at 12¾; then form top part of shoulder.

Line *C*, at 36, is the center of the breast or the breast line. The measure for this diagram was taken from the table of combined measures.

Form the balance of diagram as represented.

Add ½ of an inch to measure 11¼, 12½, 12¼, as referred to in Plate 2.

Plate 9.

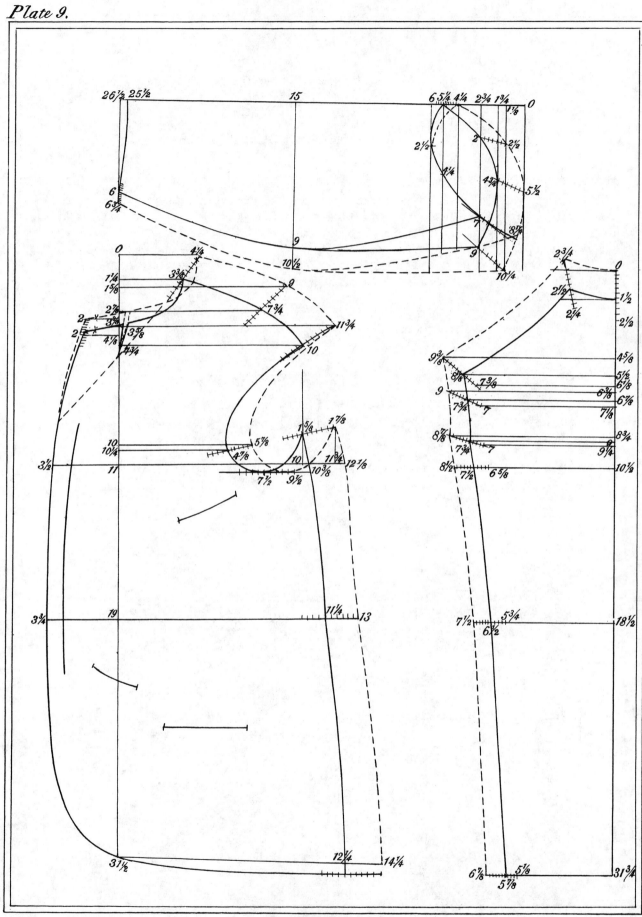

Body Sack Coat

PLATE IX.

REPRESENTS a Body Sack Coat; size 36, breast; represented by plain lines. The dotted lines represent the same style of coat, only of a larger size; being a 42 breast; said plate of diagrams being explanatory to other styles of garments comprised in this work; it also illustrates a new and novel mode of arranging a sett of patterns for various uses, which will be more fully explained as the *Geometrical Delineator*.

To fully understand its principle, and how formed, it will be necessary to produce a full sized draft of same; which can be readily done, as the distances are all illustrated by inches, marked at various points of the draft.

First, draw the perpendicular line on back; then commence at O, and mark down as given, with the inch measure the various distances; say $1\frac{1}{2}$, $2\frac{1}{2}$, etc. Square out by perpendicular line from all the points; go out on said lines as given in figures; then form curve lines as represented.

TO RECAPITULATE.

From O to $1\frac{1}{2}$, which is the distance between 36 and 42 size, is divided into 6 equal parts; each part being the different sizes, from 36 to 42; namely, 37, 38, 39, 40, 41, and from $2\frac{1}{2}$ to $2\frac{3}{4}$; from $8\frac{1}{8}$ to $9\frac{3}{8}$; from $7\frac{3}{4}$ to 9; from $7\frac{3}{4}$ to $8\frac{7}{8}$; from $7\frac{1}{2}$ to $8\frac{1}{2}$; from $6\frac{1}{2}$ to $7\frac{1}{2}$; and from $5\frac{7}{8}$ to $6\frac{7}{8}$, are divided in the same manner.

From $1\frac{1}{2}$ to $2\frac{1}{2}$, is the difference between 36 size, and 32; which is divided into 4 equal parts, which are $\frac{1}{4}$ of an inch apart, (the same as the division between 36 and 42.)

From $2\frac{1}{2}$ to $2\frac{1}{2}$; from $8\frac{1}{8}$ to $7\frac{3}{8}$; from $7\frac{3}{4}$ to 7; from $7\frac{3}{4}$ to 7; from $7\frac{1}{2}$ to $6\frac{5}{8}$; from $6\frac{1}{2}$ to $5\frac{3}{4}$; and from $5\frac{7}{8}$ to $5\frac{1}{8}$, are divided into 4 equal parts, which represent the sizes 32, 33, 34, 35; and are the same parts respectively in distance, as their correspondents from 36 to 42. It will be observed that the distance between the different points of the 36 size and 42, are unlike in almost every instance; therefore, when the different distances are found at the various points, between size 36 and 42, you are ready to diminish or increase your sizes to any limit, and they will all be of the same uniform proportion throughout; (and the same principle is found applicable to both the forepart and sleeve.) The line running from $10\frac{1}{2}$ to $6\frac{5}{8}$, $7\frac{1}{2}$, and $8\frac{1}{2}$, is the breast or balance line; and remains unchanged for all sizes, as does the back line from O to $31\frac{3}{4}$; from $10\frac{1}{2}$ to $31\frac{3}{4}$ in this draft, is the same for all sizes, but can be easily lengthened or shortened for the various sizes.

To Draft the Sleeve.

Draw the line from O to $31\frac{1}{2}$, said line being the center of breast; from 11 to 10, $11\frac{3}{4}$, and $12\frac{1}{8}$, is the balance line of the breast; said line, with the front edge of coat, remain the same on all drafts and sizes. Draw lines, and mark distances, as represented by the various figures respectively.

TO DRAFT FOREPART.

Draw line from O to $26\frac{1}{2}$; then square out at the different points, and measure off the distances as given, and form curves as represented.

The Collar on Plate 11, is to be used for this draft. It only needs one collar for the different sizes, as you have only to lengthen and shorten, to suit the neck gorge.

Plate 10.

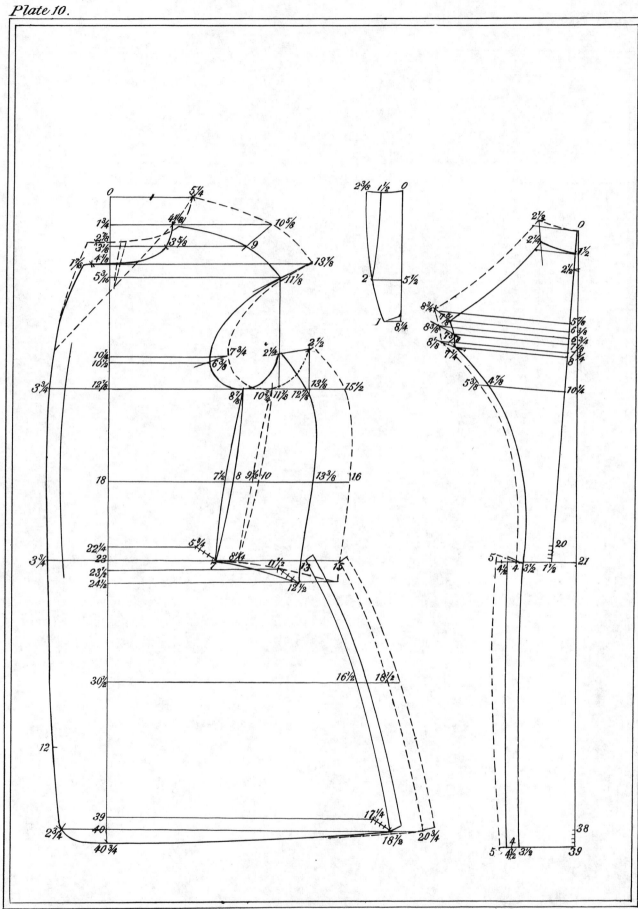

Body Paletot Coat
(see ERRATA)

PLATE X.

REPRESENTS a Boy's Paletot Coat; size, 36 breast, which is arranged to use for the same purpose as Plate 9; namely, as Geometrical Delineator, for the purpose of delineating the Body Paletot Coat, from sizes 32 to 42 breast; or larger or smaller sizes if required; and is the same principle described and illustrated on Plate 9.

To draft, draw the lines, and mark the distance from point to point, as given in inches; and you have a full size draft for practical use.

It will be noticed, that on the back, from 20 to 21, also from 38 to 39, is divided into 4 equal parts; and also on the fore-part, from 5¾ to 7; from 11½ to 12½; from 17¼ to 18½; which divisions are made for the purpose of shortening the waist and length of skirt, for sizes ranging below 36 breast: namely, 35, 34, 33, 32, which sizes require a shorter waist and skirt than the 36 size; while the sizes ranging from 36 to 42, remain the same lengths below the breast or balance line; yet the waist is lengthened, owing to the increase of length above the breast or balance line, for the different sizes.

Use the Sleeve, on Plate 14, for this coat, cutting it whole in the fore-arm.

Plate 11.

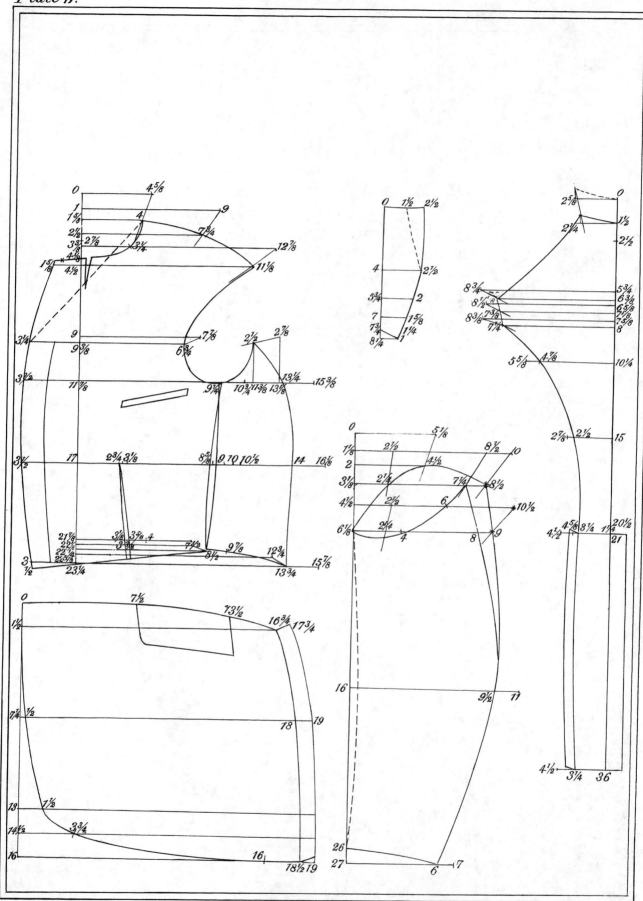

New York Walking Coat
(cutaway frock)

PLATE XI.

ON this plate we have the New York Walking Coat, with the skirt cut separate from the front of coat.

The Back, Fore-part, and Sleeve being arranged upon the Delineator plan, as has been described, while the Collar and Skirt are not; it being unnecessary, as they can be easily used for the different sizes, by shortening or lengthening, thereby saving a surplus of Patterns.

The dotted lines are not given on this Plate for the 42 size, as the figures show, at all the different points, the exact size you want to make this draft, as illustrated; being careful to have all the lines and distances marked accurately.

A back and front view of this Coat is correctly Illustrated on Frontispiece.

Plate 12.

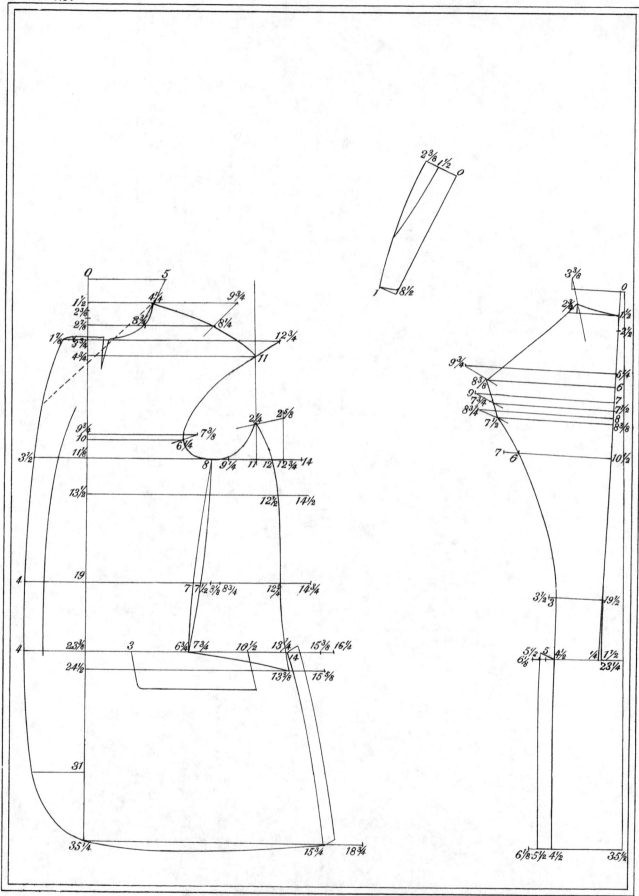

**English Walking Coat Single-Breasted
(body paletot)**

Plate 13.

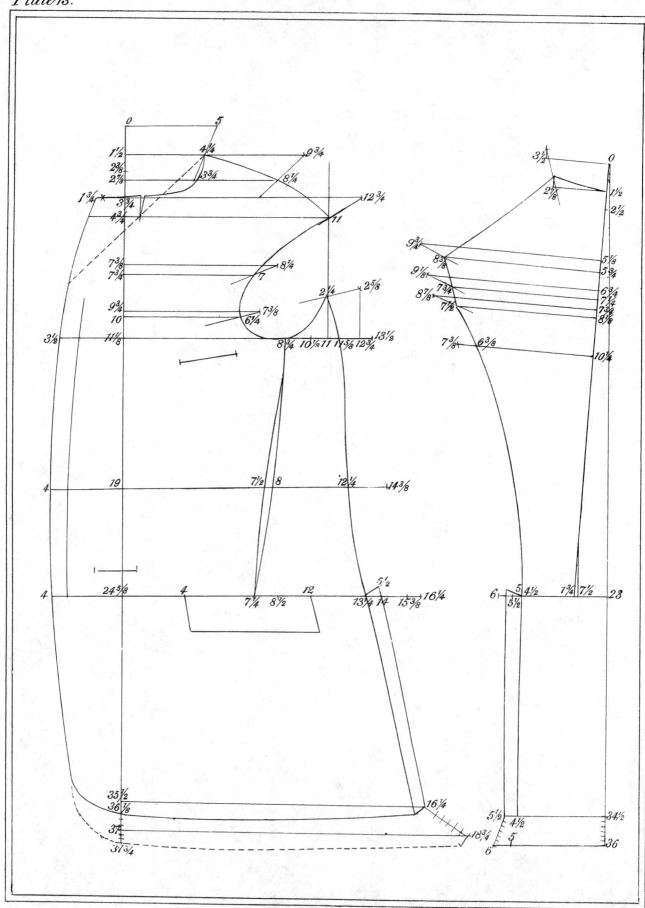

French Walking Coat Single-Breasted
(sack coat)

PLATE XII.

ON this Plate we give the Back and Fore-part of an English Walking Coat, cut Single-Breast; size 36; also arranged upon the Geometrical Delineator plan for getting up a set of Patterns.

The Back and Fore-part to be drafted as shown by the different lines and figures.

For the Sleeve, use the one given on Plate 11.

PLATE XIII.

THIS draft is upon the Geometrical Delineator plan, for a French Walking Coat, Single-breasted, size 36 breast.

Draft the Back, as shown.

From 34½ to 36, also from 5½ to 6, is divided into 6 equal parts, for the purpose of lengthening the skirt to the sizes, ranging above 36 breast, namely : 37, 38, 39, 40, 41, 42.

Draft the Fore-part, as shown.

From 36½ to 37¾, also from 16¼ to 18¾, is divided into 6 equal parts ; for sizes, from 36 to 42, breast measure.   The dotted lines give the bottom of the 42 skirt.

For the Sleeve and Collar, use those on Plate 11.

Plate 14.

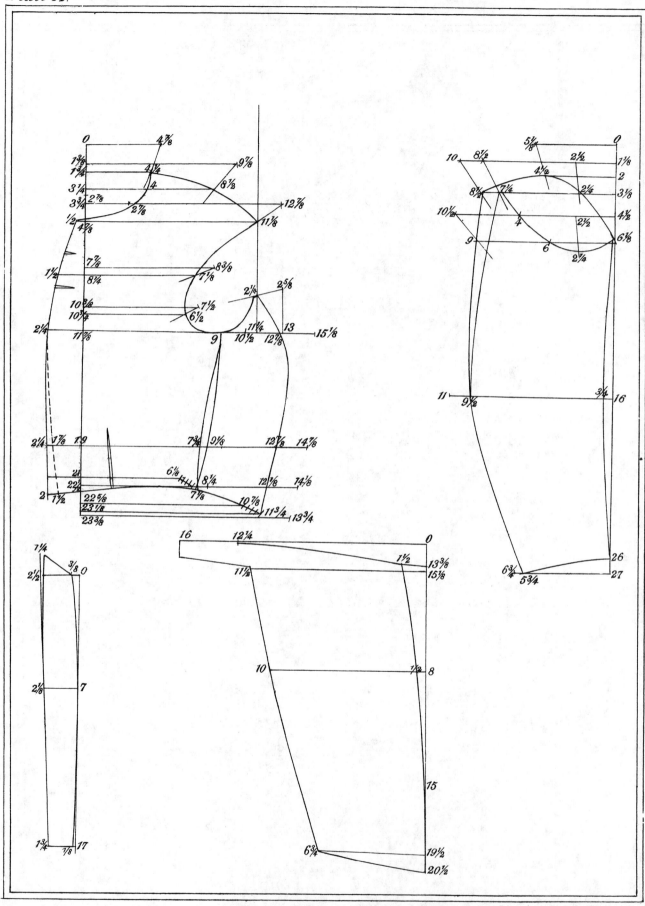

**Fore-part, Sleeve, Lapel & Skirt
(for either dress or frock coat)**

PLATE XIV.

UPON this Plate we have illustrated the Fore-part, Sleeve, Lapel and Skirt of a Dress and Frock Coat for 36 breast. To use the Fore-part for a Dress Coat, it should be cut on the front edge, as shown by the dotted lines.

To use for the D. B. Frock Coat, cut on the outside line.

From $6\frac{1}{8}$ to $7\frac{1}{8}$, also from $10\frac{7}{8}$ to $11\frac{3}{4}$ is divided into four equal parts, for sizes 35, 34, 33, 32, to give the length of waist to each.

The Sleeve can be cut whole in the Fore-arm, or hollowed $\frac{3}{4}$ inch or more, as the style may require.

The Lapel is cut as shown to use for both Frock and Dress Coats.

The Skirt is drafted for 36 size, but can be used for all sizes by changing the measure.

Use the Back and Collar found on Plate 15 for the Dress and Frock Coat.

Plate 15.

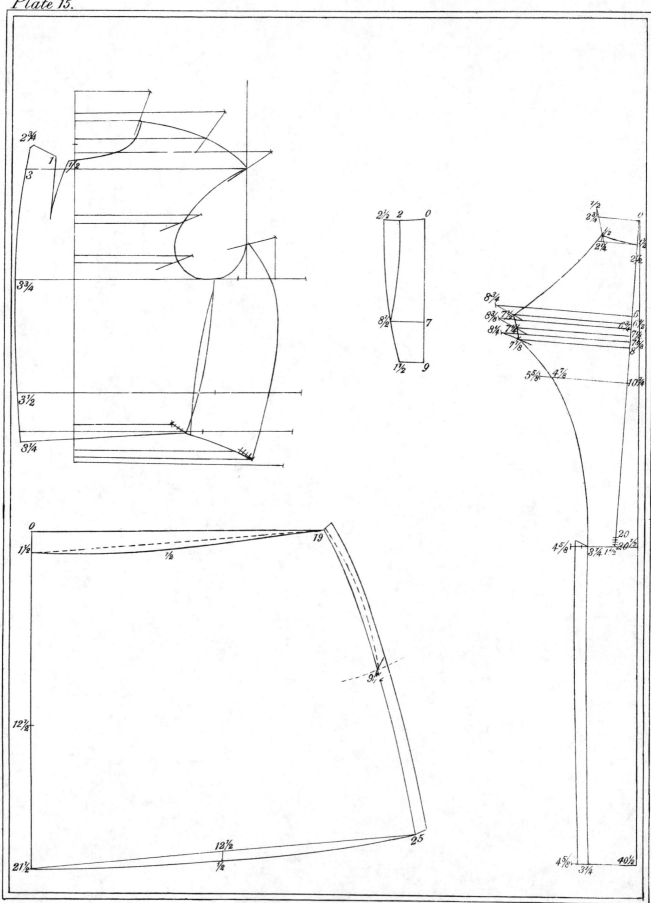

Single-Breasted Frock Coat

PLATE XV.

ON this Plate we have the full draft for a Single-Breasted Frock Coat, size 36.

The Back and Fore-part are arranged upon the Geometrical Delineator plan.

To draft the Back, proceed according to diagram.

The Fore-part is drafted the same size as the one on Plate 14, except the front, being for a different style, should be drawn as represented.

The Collar is to be drawn as shown.

The Skirt is drafted from ½ of the size of the bottom of Fore-part, with 1½ inches added for fullness in making up.

From *O* to 21½, draw a line, and square out 19 inches.

From *O*, go down on front edge 1½ inches and draw a line, as shown by the dotted line; draw curve line ½ inch below in the centre.

From *O*, mark down 12½ inches, which is two-thirds of 19½, the bottom of waist, an d from 12½ sweep dotted line, from 19 to 9½.

From 19, sweep 9½ inches, or ¼ the bottom of waist, and where sweep 9½ crosses the sweep line from 12½, is the pitch for curve to the skirt fold; form the balance as shown.

Plate 16.

Double-Breasted Paletot
(overcoat)

PLATE XVI.

ON this Plate we come to the Double-Breasted Paletot or Half-Sack Over Coat, arranged upon the *Geometrical Delineator* plan.   Size, 36 Breast.   The Back, Collar and Fore Part to be drafted as has been shown heretofore.

The Sleeve to this Coat will be found on Plate XVII.

This Style of Coat is susceptible to different changes in style of Waist and Front, also the Collar.   But it will be found that the general points of practical utility remain unchanged.

☞ TO MEASURE WITHOUT AN INSTRUMENT.

See that your customer is provided with as smooth and easy fitting Coat as possible.   Then pass the tape-measure over the outside of the Coat, standing in front of the customer, by bringing forward the hands across the shoulder-blades, close under the arm-pits, in a direct line to the center of breast, then mark top side of tape-measure, where it crosses the back-seam, also top side of the measure in front of the shoulder ; then use your wooden square to get the natural width of back, as described on Plate I, under the heading : *To Measure.*   By practice one can become expert in procuring a correct measure this way.   Nevertheless I would advise the beginner to use the square described on Plate I.

Plate 17.

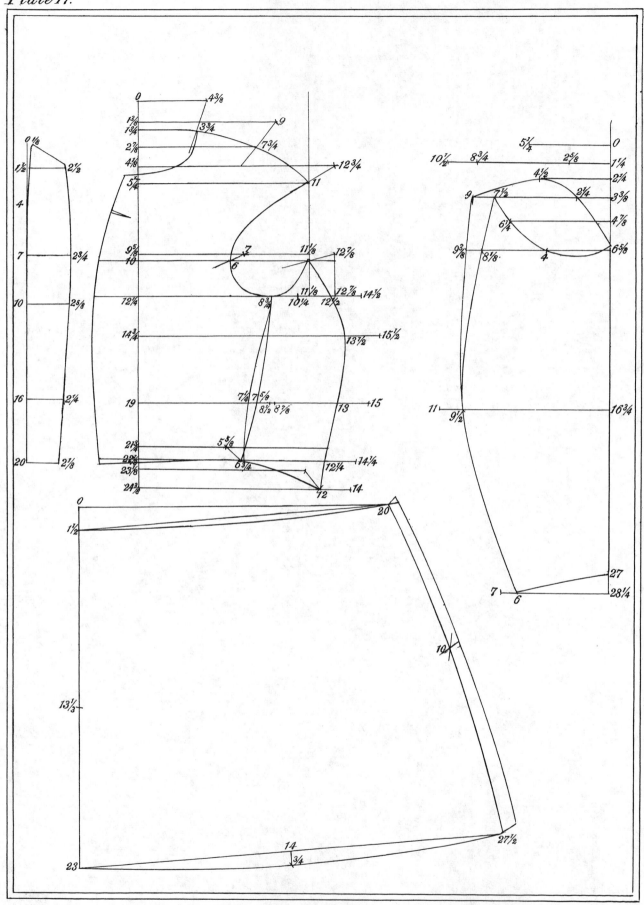

Double-Breasted Surtout Overcoat

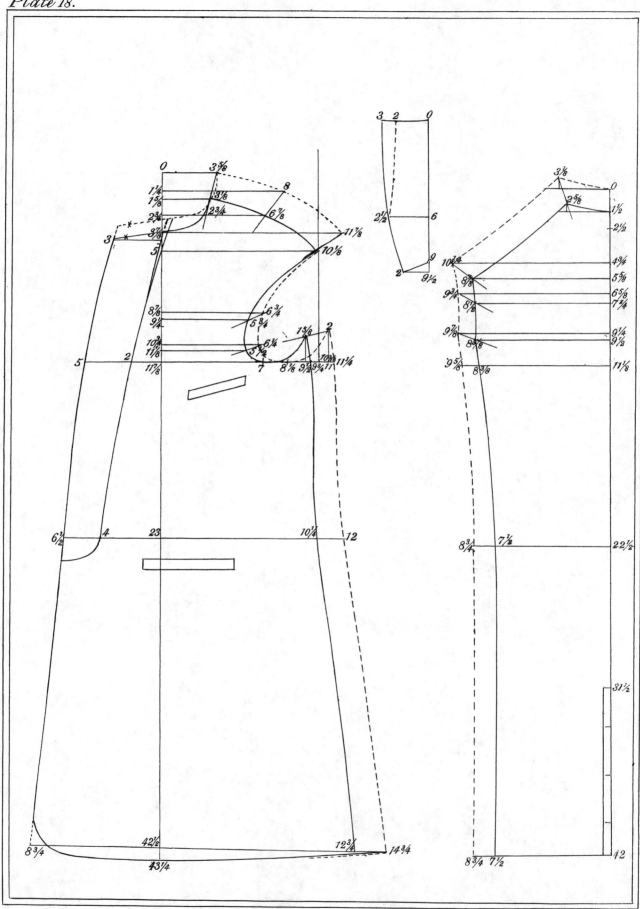

Single-Breasted Over Sack
(Chesterfield)

Plate 18.

Plate 19.

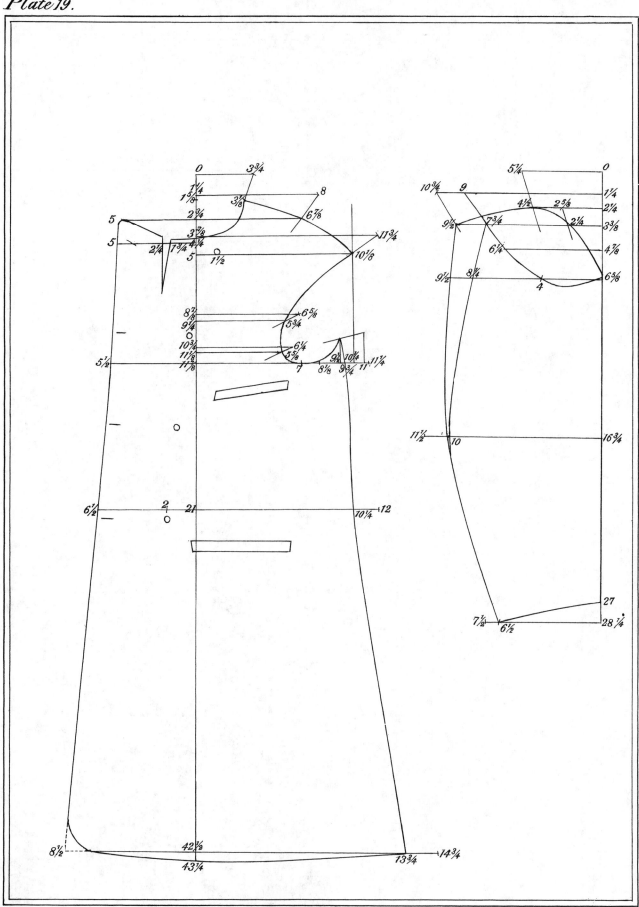

Double-Breasted Sack Overcoat
(Chesterfield)

PLATE XVII.

ON this Plate we have the Double Breasted Surtout Over Coat upon the *Delineator* plan.

The Sleeve, Fore-Part, Lapel and Skirt to be drawn as represented. It will be seen that the Skirt is drafted as described in Plate XV.

The Back of this Coat wil be found on Plate XVI.

PLATE XVIII.

WE have in this the Single-Breasted Over Sack with a Fly Front.   Size 36 Breast.

The dotted lines represent the 42 Size Breast and is arranged upon the *Geometrical Delineator* plan.

Draw as illustrated.

From 31½ to 42 is left open and made with Fly and 3 buttons or plain.

The Sleeve to this Coat will be found on Plate XIX.

PLATE XIX.

ON this Plate we have the draft for a Double-Breasted Sack Overcoat.

The Back and Collar to this Coat is found on Plate XVIII.

Plate 20.

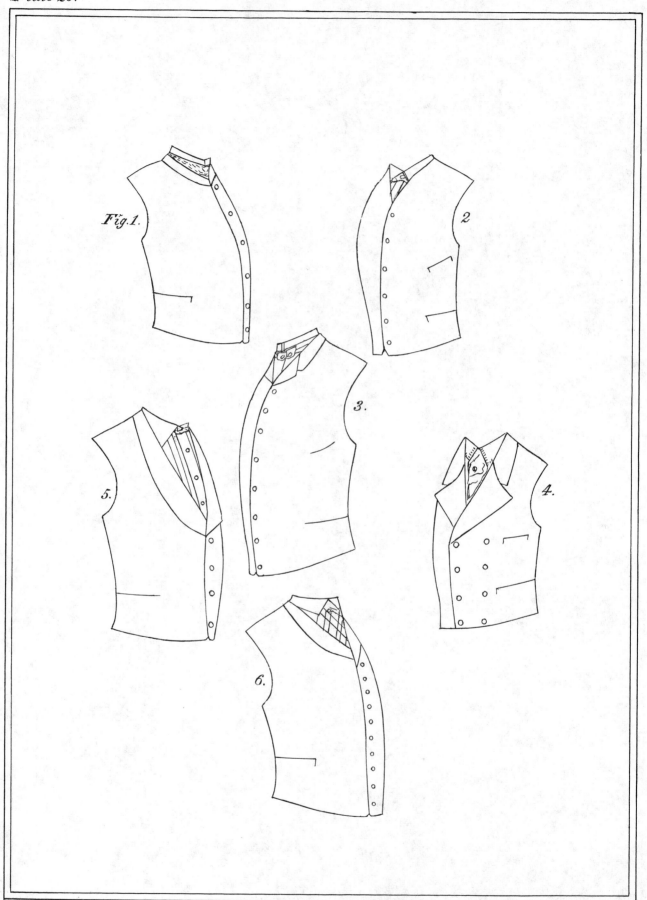

Fig.1.

2

3.

5.

4.

6.

PLATE XX.

WAISTCOAT OR VEST SYSTEM.

ON this Plate we present a view of six different styles of Vests.

FIGURE 1

Represents the Garrote Vest, cut to button up high in neck ; the collar is cut narrow.

FIGURE 2

Represents the English Walking Vest, cut to button high without a collar.

FIGURE 3

Represents a High Role Vest, buttoning up to within 3 inches of the shirt collar button ; the role to vest being cut high, say 2 inches, allows of a notch, when the collar is cut off as shown.

FIGURE 4

Represents the Double Breast, with lapel cut on, with four buttons on a side.

FIGURE 5

Represents the Shawl Form, or Low Role Vest ; wide collar, buttoning with 4 buttons, sometimes with three, and again five buttons high.

FIGURE 6

Represents the Role Collar Vest, cut to button up medium height

Plate 21.

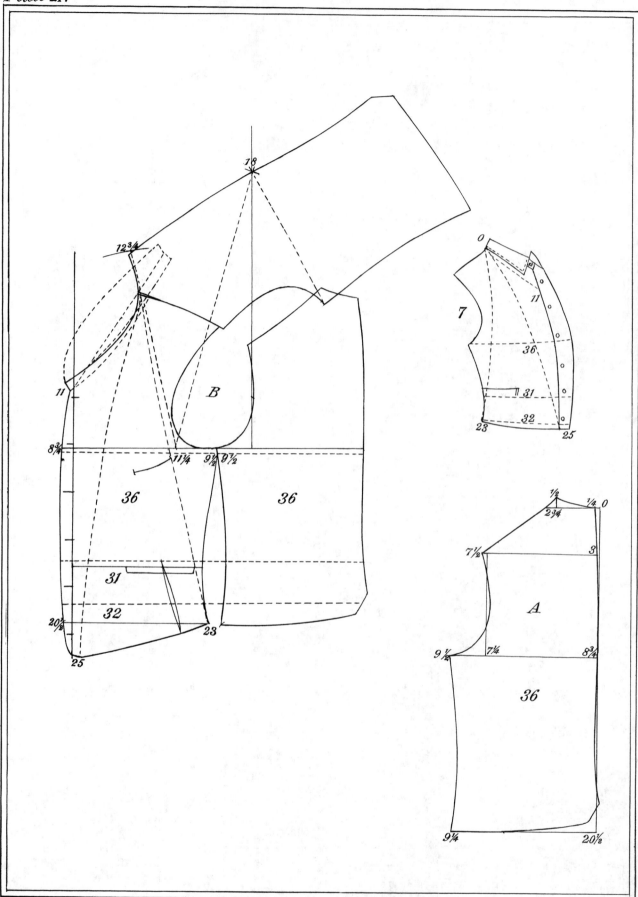

PLATE XXI.

WAISTCOAT OR VEST SYSTEM.

WHEN studying the art of cutting Vests, we should learn the well-proportiond model; in so-doing, will be better prepared to understand the different types or structures.

The measures to cut by are fully illustrated as taken and applied on Plate 21.

Figure 7 shows the *modus-operandi* of measuring for a Vest.

1st, measure from the neck joint down the front of vest 23 inches, or the necessary length.

2d, measure from neck joint, to the center of breast 11 inches, or the style of role wanted.

3d, measure down the front 25 inches, or length to suit the style.

4th, measure around the breast, passing the tape measure well up in under the arms, and across the shoulder-blades 36 inches.

5th, measure around the most hollow part of waist 31 inches.

6th, measure around the hips, or bottom of vest 32 inches.

We will commence with Back A, using the four proof measures as taken over the coat, viz. from the neck-joint, go down the back seam $8\frac{3}{4}$ inches; from front of scye over shoulder to neck-joint $12\frac{3}{4}$ inches; from same point, over shoulder to $8\frac{3}{4}$ on the back seam $17\frac{1}{4}$; from front of scye to center of back or $8\frac{3}{4}$, $11\frac{1}{4}$ inches; also the natural width of back $7\frac{1}{4}$ inches.

From O, draw line to $20\frac{1}{2}$, being $20\frac{1}{2}$ inches.

From O, go down 3 inches, or one-sixth of 18, one-half of the breast measure.

From O, apply 1st proof measure $8\frac{3}{4}$, adding $\frac{3}{4}$ of an inch, making $9\frac{1}{2}$ inches from O to $8\frac{3}{4}$.

Square out at O, 3, $8\frac{3}{4}$, and at $20\frac{1}{2}$.

From O, go in $\frac{1}{4}$ of an inch; also $2\frac{3}{4}$ of an inch, for width of back, or one-sixth of 18, $\frac{1}{2}$ of 36.

From $8\frac{3}{4}$ go in $7\frac{1}{4}$ inches, which is the natural width of back in all cases; then square up as shown.

From $8\frac{3}{4}$, measure $9\frac{1}{2}$ inches, being $\frac{1}{4}$ of 36, or the usual breast measure, with $\frac{1}{2}$ inch added, which is necessary for ease in that part of vest.

From $20\frac{1}{2}$, $9\frac{1}{4}$ inches, or to the size and shape of customer; finish curve lines as shown, going up $\frac{1}{2}$ inch from $2\frac{3}{4}$.

TO DRAFT THE FOREPART.

Draw breast line ; then lay off on said line points $8\frac{3}{4}$, $20\frac{1}{2}$, on the back, and square out. Then from $8\frac{3}{4}$, measure in $9\frac{1}{3}$, which is $\frac{1}{4}$ of 18, one-half of the breast, with $\frac{1}{2}$ inch added, (same as on back.)

Lay the back in position as shown, and from the center of back go in $11\frac{1}{4}$ inches, adding one inch, which would make $12\frac{1}{4}$ inches.

Then draw line from $7\frac{1}{4}$ (natural width of back,) to 18, (said line being the same as used in Coat drafts, to get the pitch of shoulder by.)

From $11\frac{1}{4}$, sweep front measure to neck joint $12\frac{3}{4}$ as taken.

From $11\frac{1}{4}$, sweep at 18 the measure $17\frac{1}{4}$ taken over the shoulder, adding $\frac{3}{4}$ of an inch, (in all cases.)

Place the back in position as shown, and form the curve lines to style and shape of customer.

From $12\frac{3}{4}$, or the neck joint, lay off the 1st, 2d, and 3d measures, adding seams for making, about $\frac{1}{2}$ inch.

Apply the waist and hip measures, hollowing and fishing the front to measure, giving about one inch for allowance in making up.

Draft the collar as shown by the dotted lines.

Plate 22.

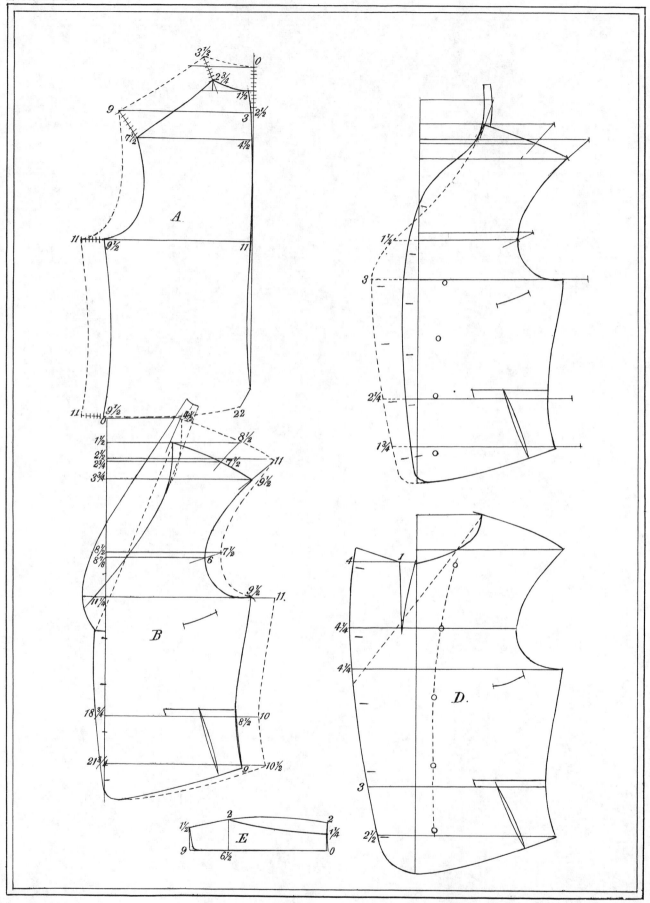

PLATE XXII.

O N this Plate we find Four Styles of Vests, viz.: Draft *B*, the Low Role or Shawl Vest, as represented on Plate 1st, Figure 5, and arranged upon the Geometrical Delineator plan.

Draft *C*, represents the English Walking Vest, the same style as found in Figure 2 ; also a Double Breasted Vest without collar.

Draft *D* is for a Double Breasted Vest with collar *E*, lapel cut on. The style is represented in Figure 4.

TO DRAFT.

Back *A*, is to be drafted as represented by the lines. The figures give the exact distance to the various points. This draft, for getting up a sett of patterns, is upon the same plan given for coats, and can be increased or diminished to any size required.

The Front *B* is drafted the same ; the plain lines give the 36 pattern ; the dotted lines the 42 size.

The Foreparts *C*, are the same size as *B*, except as shown by figures on dotted lines.

The Draft *D* is drawn for the 36 size only, but can be arranged the same as *B*, so as to cut a full sett of patterns.

Plate 23

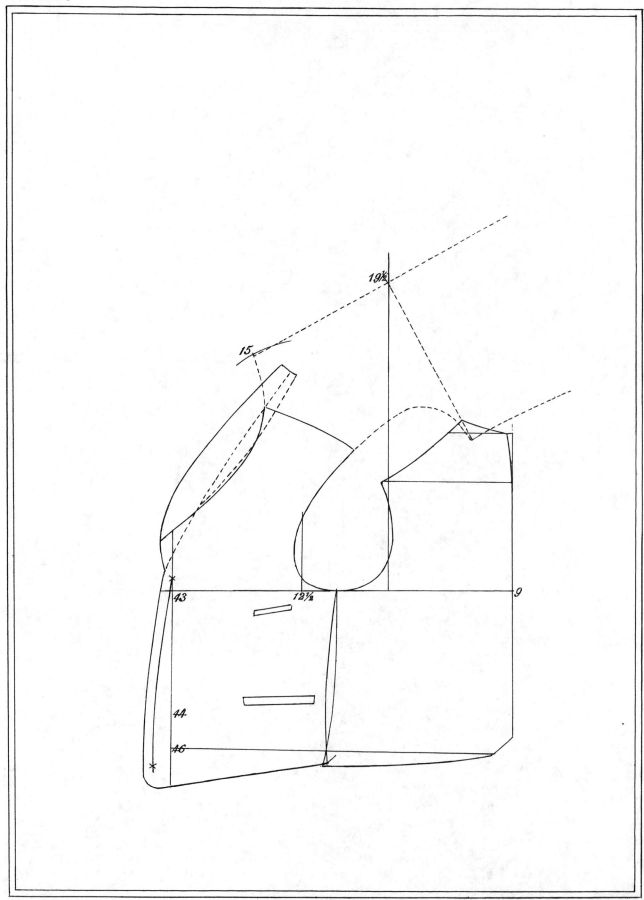

PLATE XXIII.

ON this Plate we have the draft for a corpulent man, being from the same measure as found in Plate 5, of Coat Drafts.

To draft the back, you proceed as given already on Plate 21, observing the shape, the back being wider at the bottom, owing to a large waist.

To draft the forepart, proceed as described on Plate 21, noticing that the front of forepart is extended forward of breast line, to conform to the shape; the waist being larger than the breast 3 inches.

NOTE. It would be well to produce a full sized draft, as shown in Plate 22, of the back *A*, and forepart *B*, upon heavy paper; then use some sharp point and proceed to prick off the 36 size, and with the use of that size, it will enable you to form the shape to all other sizes from 36 to 42, or from 36 to 32, thereby giving a complete sett to work from. It would be well to lay off the balance lines on each pattern, which would enable the use of said patterns for custom or shop work. Also mark on each pattern the sizes of the breast, waist, and proof measures; then you can readily find the pattern corresponding to your measure.

Plate 24.

Fig. 2.

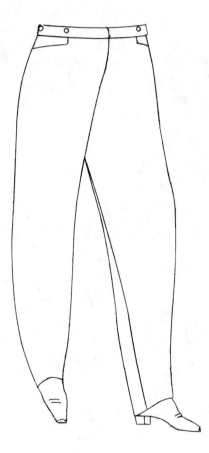

Fig. 1.

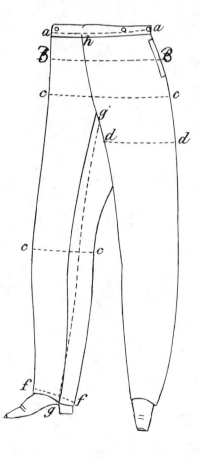

PLATE XXIV.

ON this Plate we have two Figures, representing in one, by dotted lines, the places around the lower part of the body, to get the different lengths to draw a draft for Pants.

In measuring for a pair of Pants, I would recommend the using of a Pants Rule, which will assist greatly in getting at the true height of waist, and in ruling the length of leg.

In measuring for a pair of Pants, we place the Pants Ruler as high up in the crotch at G, Figure 1, as we can conveniently, taking the length of waist from G to H, by the inches on the long arm. Then from G to G, at the heel of boot, around the waist from A to A; the hips from B to B, around the seat from C to C; around the thigh from D to D; around the knee from E to E; around the heel of boot from F to F. The Waist, Hip, and Seat Measures should be taken close; then, if necessary, give extra width in cutting.

Plate 25.

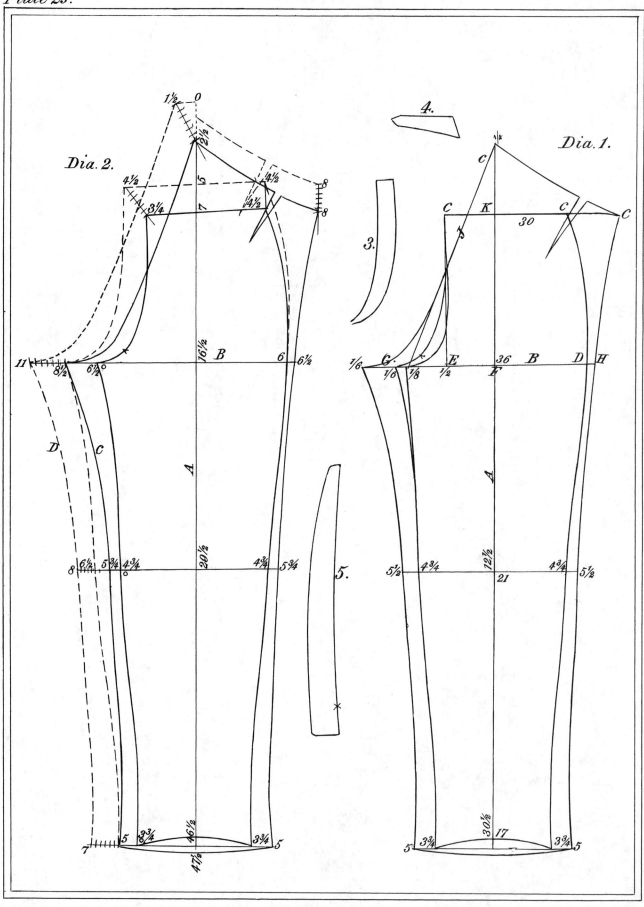

PLATE XXV.

PANTS SYSTEM.

DIAGRAM 1 represents the draft from measure, as taken on Plate 24, with the front and back in position as drawn. We will first proceed with the Forepart, as drawn on cloth.

Draw line on the edge of cloth, and square out at top.

Measure down from C to D, $9\frac{1}{2}$ inches, the length of waist.

Square out from edge of cloth at D, line B, to G.

From D to E, is $\frac{1}{2}$ of 18, one-half of 36.

From E, square up to C, by line B.

From E, go out on line B $\frac{1}{8}$, to G, one-sixth.

From G to F is one-third of 18, or 6 inches.

Square up line A, from line B, at F; then to 17.

From C to C is $\frac{1}{4}$ of 30, the waist measure.

From line B, measure down line A $12\frac{1}{2}$ to the knee; then to 17, $30\frac{1}{2}$, the length of leg.

Form lines to style and size required.

TO DRAFT THE BACK.

From G, go out one-sixth; extend line A at the top; from K, $\frac{1}{4}$ of 18, the hip measure; draw line J from $\frac{1}{8}$ on line B, to $\frac{1}{4}$, line A.

From C to C on the back, is $\frac{1}{4}$ of the waist measure, with $1\frac{1}{2}$ inches allowed for V, which cut one inch wide at the top.

From D to H, one-twelfth of eighteen.

Finish the curve lines to the body.

Form the curve lines to leg, equal distances at the knee, and bottom from line A.

Figure 3 represents the Fly cut to fit the front.

Figure 4 represents the strap.

Figure 5 represents the waist band.

Diagram 2 gives a true plan of making a sett of patterns upon the *delineator plan*.

The lines are the 36 size pattern; the dotted lines are for the 42 size.

The distances are given to every point from the 36 size in inches.

The distance between the dotted lines and plain lines are divided into 6 equal parts, the same as given for coats, ranging from 36 to 42. The smaller sizes are scaled by the same equal parts, to 32 seat measure.

Or a sett of Pants patterns can be arranged from the following measures, using the 36 pattern to form curves by, having the same length for all sizes above 36, which is a convenient way, as the lengths are easily changed on the cloth.

10, length of waist 12½ to knee, 30½ full length.

30, waist, 36 seat measure.

31, " 37 " " 29 waist, 35 seat measure.

32, " 38 " " 28 " 34 " "

33, " 39 " " 27 " 33 " "

34, " 40 " " 26 " 32 " "

35, " 41 " "

36, " 42 " " cutting the length of waist 9½, knee 12, length 29, below 36 size, and you have a convenient sett of sizes.

Plate 26.

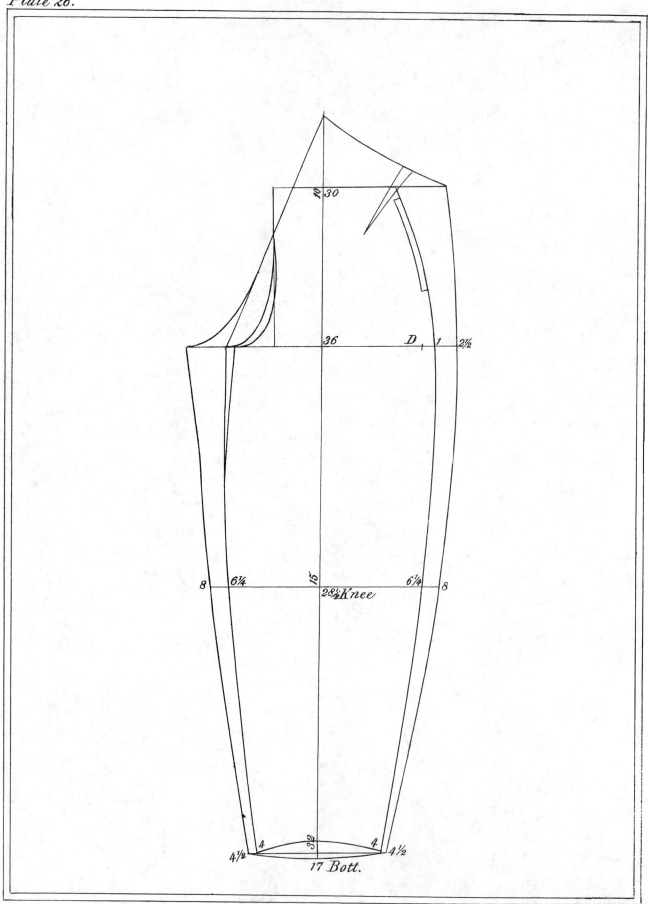

Plate 27.

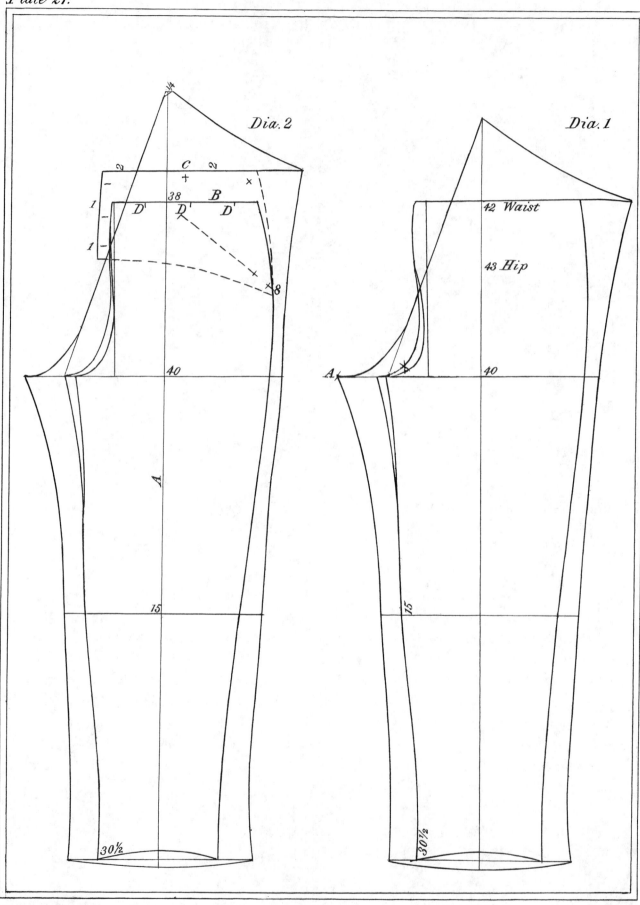

Dia. 2

Dia. 1

42 Waist

43 Hip

PLATE XXVI.

ON this Plate we give the full Leg and Hip Pants, to be drafted the same as given in Diagram 1, Plate 25, except the sizes around the hips and knee, which are given in inches on the Plate.

PLATE XXVII.

WE have on this Plate two styles of Pants for the stout waist. Diagram 1 is a draft for the corpulent waist; the curve lines bring out the shape to correspond to the measures. In other respects, we proceed as has been given, noticing this fact, that the stout built man needs more length at point A, from 1 to 3 inches, than a thin man.

Diagram 2. We have a draft for a pair of Whole Falls, or Fall Front Pants, cut for a stout waist; they are cut like ordinary pants, except the top part of the back.

From line B, go up 2 inches; square across, as shown for the lap pieces and the back.

From line E, go up $\frac{1}{4}$ of 20; form the front of laps 1 inch front of the forepart, marking 3 buttons on same; d, d, d, are the button-holes, or fall pieces, or the fronts. There should be buttons on the laps to correspond. Said Laps are cut 5 inches wide in front, 8 inches on the side. See dotted lines. There wants to be a facing to the fall pieces to come down and across, as shown by the dotted line, the size of front. It needs no waistband or flys to this style of Pants. The Pocket is worked across the Laps, as shown.

Measure	42	41	40	39	38	37	36	35	34	33	32
BREAST MEASURE.	42	41	40	39	38	37	36	35	34	33	32
WAIST MEASURE.	38	37	36	35	34	33	32	31	30	29	28
FIRST MEASURE ON THE BACK.	$10\frac{1}{4}$	10	$9\frac{3}{4}$	$9\frac{1}{2}$	$9\frac{1}{4}$	9	$8\frac{3}{4}$	$8\frac{1}{2}$	$8\frac{1}{4}$	8	$7\frac{3}{4}$
LENGTH OF NATURAL WAIST.	$18\frac{1}{2}$	$18\frac{1}{4}$	18	$17\frac{3}{4}$	$17\frac{1}{2}$	$17\frac{1}{4}$	17	$16\frac{3}{4}$	$16\frac{1}{2}$	$16\frac{1}{4}$	16
MEASURE FROM FRONT OF SCYE TO NECK JOINT.	$14\frac{1}{4}$	14	$13\frac{3}{4}$	$13\frac{3}{8}$	13	$12\frac{5}{8}$	$12\frac{1}{4}$	$11\frac{7}{8}$	$11\frac{1}{2}$	$11\frac{1}{8}$	$10\frac{3}{4}$
MEASURE FROM THE FRONT OF SCYE OVER THE SHOULDER TO FIRST MEASURE ON BACK.	$19\frac{1}{2}$	$19\frac{1}{8}$	$18\frac{3}{4}$	$18\frac{3}{8}$	18	$17\frac{5}{8}$	$17\frac{1}{4}$	$16\frac{3}{4}$	$16\frac{3}{8}$	16	$15\frac{5}{8}$
MEASURE FROM THE FRONT OF SCYE TO THE CENTRE OF BACK.	$12\frac{3}{4}$	$12\frac{1}{2}$	$12\frac{1}{4}$	12	$11\frac{3}{4}$	$11\frac{1}{2}$	$11\frac{1}{4}$	11	$10\frac{3}{4}$	$10\frac{1}{2}$	$10\frac{1}{4}$
ELIPTIC, OR THE MEASURE FROM FRONT OF SCYE TO THE NATURAL WAIST ON BACK SEAM.	$13\frac{1}{2}$	$13\frac{3}{8}$	$13\frac{1}{4}$	13	$12\frac{3}{4}$	$12\frac{1}{2}$	$12\frac{1}{4}$	12	$11\frac{3}{4}$	$11\frac{1}{2}$	$11\frac{1}{4}$
SCYE.	$18\frac{3}{4}$	$18\frac{3}{8}$	$17\frac{7}{8}$	$17\frac{1}{2}$	17	$16\frac{5}{8}$	$15\frac{3}{4}$	$15\frac{1}{4}$	$14\frac{3}{4}$	$14\frac{1}{4}$	$13\frac{3}{4}$
NATURAL WIDTH OF BACK STROP.	$8\frac{3}{4}$	$8\frac{1}{8}$	$7\frac{7}{8}$	$7\frac{5}{8}$	$7\frac{1}{2}$	$7\frac{3}{8}$	$7\frac{1}{4}$	$7\frac{1}{8}$	7	$6\frac{3}{4}$	$6\frac{1}{2}$
MEASURE TO THE ELBOW.	$23\frac{3}{8}$	$22\frac{3}{4}$	$22\frac{1}{4}$	$21\frac{3}{4}$	$21\frac{1}{4}$	$20\frac{3}{4}$	$20\frac{1}{4}$	$19\frac{3}{4}$	$19\frac{1}{4}$	$18\frac{3}{4}$	$18\frac{1}{4}$
FULL LENGTH OF SLEEVE.	35	$34\frac{1}{2}$	34	$33\frac{1}{2}$	33	$32\frac{1}{2}$	32	$31\frac{1}{2}$	31	$30\frac{1}{2}$	30
GORGE MEASURE.	$10\frac{1}{4}$	10	$9\frac{3}{4}$	$9\frac{1}{2}$	$9\frac{1}{4}$	9	$8\frac{3}{4}$	$8\frac{1}{2}$	$8\frac{1}{4}$	8	$7\frac{3}{4}$

PROOF MEASURES.

Table of Combined Measures

FOR CUTTING COAT PATTERNS.

ITS USE.

IRST, you can make a set of Patterns from 32 to 42 breast, that is the Back and Front or Fore-part of Coat, as shown on Plate 8, drawing all the lines on same, as you draft, and marking on each pattern the lengths, proof-measures and sizes around ; then make a collar and skirt pattern to use for the set, which are all that are needed, for they can be easily enlarged or diminished for all sizes on the cloth—it will save having so many extra patterns. Then make the Sleeve Patterns for each, marking the sizes on each. Now to use for custom work, you look on the Table of Combined Measures for the proof measures that correspond with the proof measures on your Cutting-book ; paying no attention to the size of breast measure. When found, take the pattern made from the same measures and you are ready to draft your coat on cloth, saving a good deal of time. Providing you do not find the proof measures on the table to correspond with your Cutting-book, use the one next nearest, for it will be easy to change on the cloth the different parts, and still keep the proper balance ; or should you wish, you can make the full set on one pattern as described on page 111.

TO CUT OVER GARMENTS.

IT is only necessary to use the Under-coat measure, adding to certain measures the proper allowance for making up and the real difference existing between the two garments, viz: the Under and Over-coat.

Add to first measure, from neck joint 8¾, ½ inch for the Surtout or Dress Over-coat, and for Sack Over-coat add ¾ of an inch to 8¾.

Add one inch to the measure front of scye to the neck joint, and for Sacks 1¼ inches.

Add ½ inch to the measure from front of scye over the shoulder to first measure on back, for Sacks ¾ of an inch.

Add one inch to the measure from front of scye to center of back, 1¼ inches for Sacks.

Add one inch to the eliptic, or measure from front of scye to natural waist.

Add to the full width of back strop ½ or 1 inch, or as much as you deem necessary, leaving the natural width the same to draw line *A* by.

Add 1 inch to the scye measure.

Add 1 inch to the full length of Sleeve, including the width of back.

Add ½ inch to the neck gorge measure.

Add 2 inches to the full breast measure.

Add 2 inches to the full waist measure.

THE GEOMETRICAL DELINEATOR.

TO more fully understand the benefits arising from this system of getting up Patterns, I will give the way of producing a Sett of Patterns to be on one sheet, as given on Plate 9, 10, 11, etc., of the different styles, and with both described so plain, besides being illustrated, one cannot fail to understand, how to form and use the *Delineator* for any style of Coat. First draft the back for a Frock Coat (as shown on Plate 8) from the 36 Breast measure; then draft from the 42 Breast measure another back, the same style, laying the 36 size on said 42, so that the back line of each lay together; also the balance from 8¾, and 10¼ together; then draw short lines at the different points, as seen on Plate 14, using the 36 size to form the curve lines to the different sizes.

THE FOREPART.

Draft the 36 size as shown on Plate 8; then draft the 42 size, using the same centre of breast on line *B*; also the front line or curve to breast; then draw the lines, and mark the distances from the 42 proof measure, and finish as shown by the draft on Plate 14. Proceed to divide the distance between the 36 and 42, into 6 equal parts at the different points; proceed with the sleeve the same, and you have the sett complete on one sheet. Now mark at the division of parts the different size coats or breast measure, and punch holes for each size; then cut around the 42 size, so as to use the curve lines to form the different sizes by; you then lay your pattern on the cloth, and mark at the different points the size required, then you use the curves to the 42, to form said draft, thereby preserving the same style of coat for each size. Proceed with all styles the same.

Additional Illustrations

Gentleman's Magazine   1860

Gentleman's Magazine   1860

Gentleman's Magazine   1860

Gentleman's Magazine 1861

Gentleman's Magazine 1861

Gentleman's Magazine   1861

(unknown French Magazine) 1861

Gentleman's Magazine   1861

Gentleman's Magazine 1862

Gazette of Fashion 1862

Gentleman's Magazine   1862

Gazette of Fashion 1862

Gazette of Fashion 1863

Gazette of Fashion   1863

Gazette of Fashion 1863

Gazette of Fashion   1863

Gazette of Fashion 1863

Gazette of Fashion   1863

Gazette of Fashion   1863

Gazette of Fashion   1864

Gazete of Fashion   1864

Gazette of Fashion 1864

Gazette of Fashion   1864

January 1864

Gazette of Fashion   1864

139

Frank Leslie's Illustrated 1865

Great Base Ball Match between The Atlantic and Eckford clubs of Brooklyn,

at the Union Base Ball Grounds, Brooklyn.

140

Tailor & Cutter   1868

Portrait of Fashion,

LORD STANLEY.

Tailor & Cutter   1868

Tailor & Cutter   1869

Tailor & Cutter 1869

144

Tailor & Cutter 1869

Tailor & Cutter   1869

Tailor & Cutter   1869

Boy's Clothing

Boy's Clothing

In today's children's clothing gender differences are stressed very early. Boy's might be dress in 'outfits' at a very early age, but they are usually fairly macho. The local children's clothing store says that up to age 3 - 4 boys wear very practical clothing and/or fancy dress like: western, sailor, tuxedos, etc. From age 5 on they mirror what is happening in the adult male world stressing casual, easy to take care of, ply-wear. This might mirror baseball, 'grung', football, jogging, sweat-pants, etc. There are also more formal suits worn by some boys to church, weddings, parties, etc.

In Victorian times, and in this case the 1860s, we can see a similar pattern except that all children, regardless of gender, wore dresses or smocks until they were around 5 years old. There are examples of these and instructions and/or patterns in both *Civil war Ladies* and Hartley's *The Ladies' Hand Book of Fancy & Ornamental Work*.

At around 5 years old boys wore 'outfits', or clothes that reflected the fashions of the times and the social status of their parents. Examples of these, including a boy's Zouave jacket (a reflection of adult military fashion), will be found with patterns in Devere's *The Handbook of Practical Cutting on the Centre Point System*. An interesting illustration of a boy in a Zouave outfit can be found in the illustrations of the *N.Y. 7th Regiment* section and another in the 1861 section of *Additional Illustrations*.

The examples which follow from *Civil War Ladies* do not follow adult fashions, but were children's fashions or 'outfits'. Nearly every month covered in *Civil War Ladies* shows children's fashions, both boy's and girl's from Peterson's Magazine.

Boy's clothing, like everything else in fashion, has to be judged by both social and geographic factors. A boy on the farm will probably not wear the same clothing as one in the city unless he has a good outfit for special occasions. At the same time, boys in the city will differ depending upon their social status. During this time there was also a certain amount of backlash against the tide of new immigrants. This shows up in the attitudes towards some of the special military units formed by immigrants, and it can also be seen in people's attitudes towards children whose

150

clothing was 'un-American' (even though 'American' fashion was really English or French). As always fashion magazines will not give illustrations of, nor patterns for, the more commonplace and poorer people's clothing. Peterson's Magazine is fairly middle-class and for those striving to be middle-class. Godey's Lady's Book is a step above that and shows upper middle-class clothing. English tailoring magazines like Tailor & Cutter, which were extensively used by American tailors, have patterns and illustrations which reflect those worn more by upper class boys.

In looking at the visual records of the times, both drawings and photographs, it can be seen that, depending upon the situation, boy's clothing, like men's, can take a wide variety of forms. Unless it is a posed, formal situation, the clothing will probably be much more relaxed than anything found in a fashion magazine.

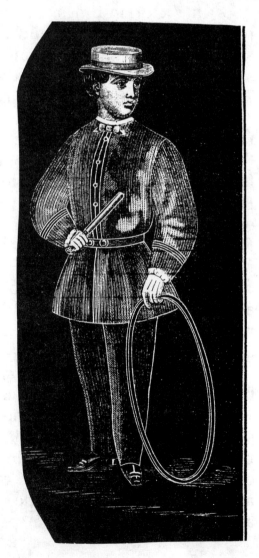

BOYS' SEA SIDE DRESS.

THE figure on plate 2 represents a dress peculiarly adapted at the present season for sea-side wear. It is generally termed a "Loose Blouse" or "Norfolk Shirt." It is a garment in no way restraining the free motion of the wearer, and in no way liable to have its appearance spoilt by any disarrangement to which it may be subjected. It can also be made of any material, from brown holland to the finest cloth, and ornamented to any degree desirable.

To many the cutting of these and similar garments are a difficulty. They, however, may be easily produced from any loose cut garment, such as a three seam jacket or a Chesterfield; all the deviation necessary is to increase the width of back and fore-part on the side-seams and before and behind; raise the gorge in front and sink the centre of back, and raise the shoulder points of both back and fore-part. The changes in gorge and shoulder will enable the extra width given to fall equally all round, and give the ease and grace so essential to the comfort and appearance of these garments.

Tailor and Cutter 1869

Boy's Dress (2 1/2 years old)
Peterson's Magazine 1864

The diagram for this popular dress (for which see next page), gives the proper dimensions for the complete dress to fit a boy two and a half years old. The dress is to be made of gray silk poplin, trimmed with black or very dark blue velvet ribbon two inches in width. The front is in one entire piece, opening diagonally from A to B, closing with hooks and loops at the shoulder, or with a button corresponding with those upon the strap reaching from the shoulder

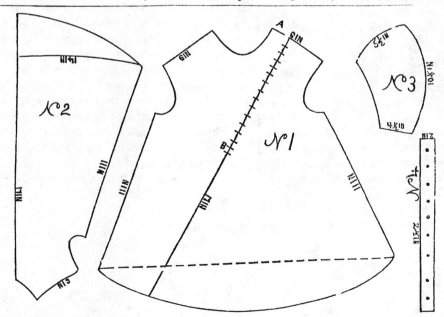

to the bottom of the dress. It is very simple and easily made: in fact, only a loose blouse, confined at the waist with a leather or velvet belt, and large buckle.

No. 1. FRONT.
No. 2. HALF OF BACK.
No. 3. SLEEVE.
No. 4. STRAP FROM SHOULDER.

SAILOR KNICKERBOCKER-SUIT.

BY EMILY H. MAY.

In addition to the engravings of children's fashions, given in the front of the number, we print here an illustration of a "Sailor's Knicker-bocker-Suit" for a boy from four to six years

old, accompanying it, on the next page, by a diagram, from which it may be cut out. We have so often given directions for enlarging these diagrams, and cutting out a paper pattern of the full size from them, that we deem it unnecessary to repeat them here.

This style of dress is very fashionable in Paris, at the present season, for boys. Our pattern consists of a jacket, with lapels in front, and a pair of Knickerbockers.

No. 1. FRONT OF JACKET.
No. 2. HALF OF BACK OF JACKET.
No. 3. HALF OF SLEEVE.
No. 4. ONE FRONT OF KNICKERBOCKER.
No. 5. ONE BACK OF KNICKERBOCKER.

The front of the Knickerbocker may be distinguished from the back by being shorter, and the knee from the waist by being narrower. The outside seam of the Knickerbocker must be joined to within five inches of the top. The inside seam, which is sloped, must be joined as far as the point. Each leg is gathered into a band, which is worn below the knee. The legs are made first, then joined together down the center of both back and front. A band, two inches wide, must be added, according to the size of the waist; one half of the band is for the front, the other half for the back; the Knickerbockers fasten at the sides. Pockets may be added at the sides, if desired. The back and front must each be pleated with three small pleats into the band.

The jacket is turned back in front with lapels,

and should be stitched at the top into a narrow, straight collar. The lapels are made of the same material as the jacket. The sleeve pattern represents both the front and back of sleeve; the smaller half being the front.

For evening wear, this suit should be made of black velvet, and trimmed with jet "Tom Thumb" fringe; scarlet silk stockings and a scarlet neck-tie completing the costume. The shirt should be made either of cambric or fine linen, with full embroidered front and collar.

For morning wear, cloth is the more appropriate material; a linen shirt, with plain linen collar, should replace the embroidery; bright blue, violet, or scarlet neck-tie and stockings.

Our sketch represents a boy wearing this costume. The small cap is of black velvet, bordered with Astrakan fur, and ornamented with a red feather; Polish kid boots with tassels, and red spun silk stockings.

We have seen several descriptions of cloth, which are suitable for this suit; the usual width is three-quarters of a yard, and three yards would be required. The tweeds occasionally run double-width; then, of course, half the above quantity would be found sufficient.

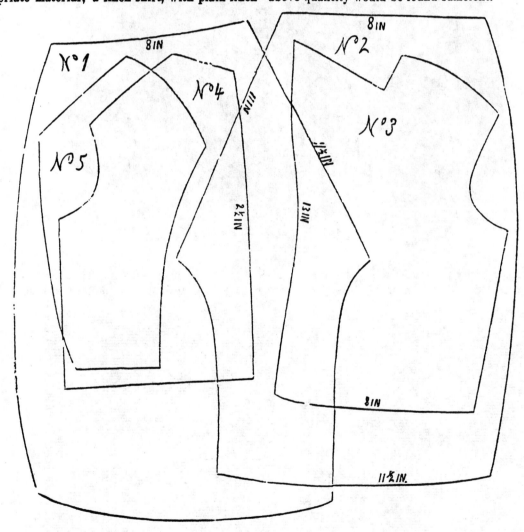

Peterson's Magazine 1866

154

LOOSE JACKET AND WAISTCOAT FOR BOY.

BY EMILY H. MAY.

This is a pretty pattern for a boy of three or four years old. The material may be any sort of cloth suitable for the season. The sleeve is arranged with a turned-back cuff, as will be

BRAIDING DESIGN FOR THE TURNED-BACK CUFF AND WAISTCOAT.

Peterson's Magazine 1861

BRAIDING DESIGN FOR TRIMMING ROUND THE JACKET.

seen in the illustration, and the waistcoat is stitched in the seams under the arms, so forming one garment. The broad braiding design which we also give is for trimming round the jacket,

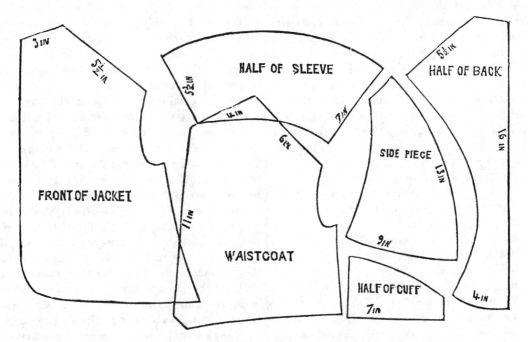

DIAGRAM FOR CUTTING OUT JACKET AND WAISTCOAT.

and the narrow one for the turned back cuff and waistcoat. The braiding design would be equally suitable for ladies' loose or tight jackets. We annex also a diagram by which to cut it out.

THE KNICKERBOCKER SUIT.

BY EMILY H. MAY.

THE Knickerbocker costume is now the favorite style of dress for boys, when they are of that awkward age, too young to be breeched, and too old to wear frocks and pinafores. This costume has a great many recommendations: it can be made in almost any material; it always looks neat and tidy; and for the play-ground is peculiarly suitable, as it leaves boys the free use of their limbs, besides being rather more manly than petticoats, which used to be (particularly at school) a boy's abhorrence. The suit we have illustrated is made of cloth for winter wear. On the next page we give a diagram, as follows:

No. 1. BACK OF KNICKERBOCKERS.
No. 2. FRONT OF KNICKERBOCKERS.
No. 3. HALF OF BACK OF JACKET.
No. 4. FRONT OF JACKET.
No. 5. HALF OF BACK OF WAISTCOAT.
No. 6. FRONT OF WAISTCOAT.
No. 7. SLEEVE.
No. 8. CUFF AND SLEEVE.
No. 9. POCKET FOR KNICKERBOCKERS.

THE JACKET is bound at the edges with broad braid, and is trimmed above that with two rows of narrow; whilst down the front, on each side, nineteen round and stout buttons are placed at regular distances, the jacket being merely fastened with a hook and eye at the top. The back is cut in one piece, with a seam down the middle, and each of the fronts has a pocket put in, bound with braid and trimmed with two rows of the narrow braid; a line, showing where the pocket should be put, is drawn in the diagram. The sleeves are made with a seam at the elbow, and with a turned-back cuff, also bound and trimmed; the line crossing the top of the sleeve indicates where the front half should be sloped at the top.

THE WAISTCOAT.—The fronts are made of cloth, bound and trimmed with braid, and are fastened with ten buttons and button holes. A piece of broad braid, doubled, is run on, to imitate a pocket, with a row of narrow braid run round it in the shape of the line shown in the diagram. The back is made in one piece, of double dark twill, and, in joining the back to the front, the seam is left open as far as the letter A, to give the waistcoat a little play in front, and make it sit well over the stomach. The back has two strings to tie it in behind to the size required.

THE KNICKERBOCKERS.—Each leg is cut in one piece, that is to say, there is no seam down the straight part; but it should be opened as far as the two B's, and a false hem made on each side of the opening. This straight part is trimmed with three straps of broad braid, with a button in the center, the braid being put on in a point at each end. The top of the Knickerbockers is gathered into a band, the length of the band being eleven inches and a half in front, and twelve inches and a half behind, to allow for buttoning over, and each of the bands has three button holes made in them of rather a large size. The bottom of the Knickerbockers is plainly hemmed with a hem half an inch wide, in which a piece of broad elastic should be put, so as to make them fit tightly to the leg, and this elastic should always be taken out, if the suit is to be washed. The pocket shown in the diagram is put in on the right side of the Knickerbockers, and the opening in it should be made as far as the cross. All these three patterns are drawn without allowing for turnings anywhere, or for the hem at the bottom of the trousers. In former numbers, we have explained how to enlarge these patterns.

157

DIAGRAM FOR KNICKERBOCKER SUIT.

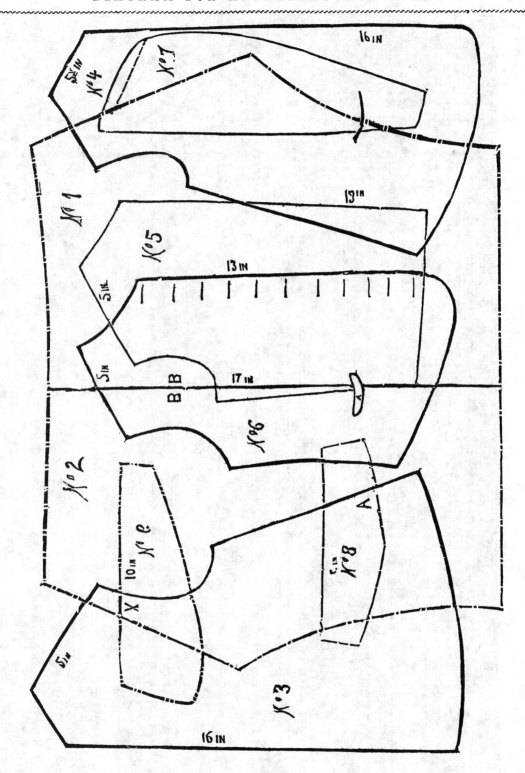

Peterson's Magazine 1861

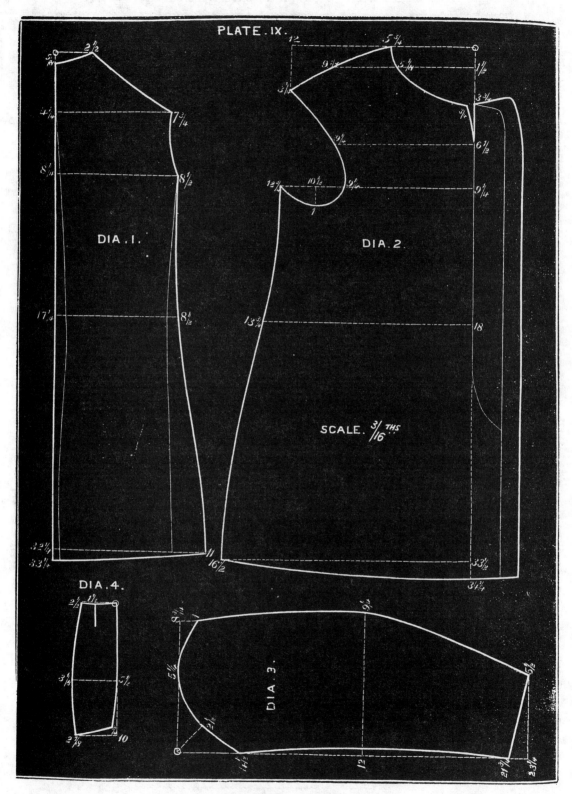

Boy's Over-coat
Tailor and Cutter 1869

Boy's Over-coat

The fine lines on our diagrams show the alteration required to produce a Chesterfield. The fore-part is untouched, but the back is slightly hollowed at back seam, and about two inches taken off the side gradually from the top through the bottom. Vents may either be left at the sides, or a single one at the back.

By taking an inch or inch and a half off the width of lapel, the single breast is obtained, though for boys the double-breasted is much to be preferred, especially when made in a nice, neat make of Harrington or Elysian, which are materials better adapted for boys' over-coats than anything else. Blues or blacks, or an Oxford mixture, are the best colors for boys' over-coats. We do not consider it is consistent with good taste to dress young boys in brown or olive, or green, and advise our readers never to recommend it. To produce the pattern to its original size, take the 15 1/2 graduated tape, commencing with

The Back, Plate 9, Diagram 1
Draw a line for back seam, and mark down from the angle 0 5/8, 4 1/4, 8 1/4, 17 1/4, 32 1/4, and 33 1/4; draw the square lines, and mark on them 2 1/2, 7 3/4, 8 1/2, 8 1/2, and 11, then complete the outline thus indicated.

The Fore-part, Diagram 2
Draw a square line from 0, allowing 3 to 3 1/2 inches for width of lapel; mark down from 0 1 1/2, 3 3/4, 6 1/2, 9 1/4, 18, 33 1/2, 34 1/4; draw cross lines, and mark the widths on them 5 3/4, 12, from 12 down 3 1/4; then 5 1/8, 9 3/4, 9 1/4, 9 1/4, 10, 12 3/4, 13 3/4, 16; form the fore-part by these points, hollowing the side from 12 3/4 to 13 3/4, and adding a gentle round to 16 1/2 at bottom; take out 3/4 at neck, and from the front to style required, or as per diagram.

Tailor and Cutter 1869

The Sleeve, Diagram 3
Draw right angle, marking down 4 1/2, 12, 21 3/4, 23 1/4, across 2 1/2, 5 1/4, 8 3/4(1), 9 1/4, 5 1/2.

The Collar, Diagram 4
Mark 5 1/2 and 10 as lengths, and 1 1/2, 2 1/2, 3 1/8, 2 7/8 as depths, taking off 3/4 at 10; stretch both sewing on edge and fall, till it sets close round the top and free on the shoulders. Velvet is indispensable to a neat finish, and enhances the appearance and value in the customer's eye - thing every wise tailor will endeavor to accomplish.

Peterson's Magazine 1866

LITTLE BOY'S JACKET.

BY EMILY H. MAY.

THIS neat little affair is made of a plain-colored cashmere, and is trimmed with blue velvet, or blue cashmere. It is cut, in the back, exactly as in front, only a little shorter. The sleeve is open for a little distance on the back.

No. 1. ONE FRONT.

No. 2. HALF THE BACK.

No. 3. HALF THE SLEEVE.

No. 4. STRAP FOR SLEEVE AND FRONT.

This makes a very pretty jacket, at a small expense, and with comparatively little trouble.

The accompanying diagram will more fully and clearly explain the arrangement for cutting the jacket. In our next number we will give a design for a little boy's pantaloons, and accompany it with a diagram. The two together will make a very neat and becoming suit.

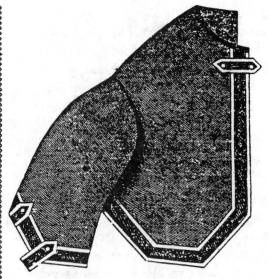

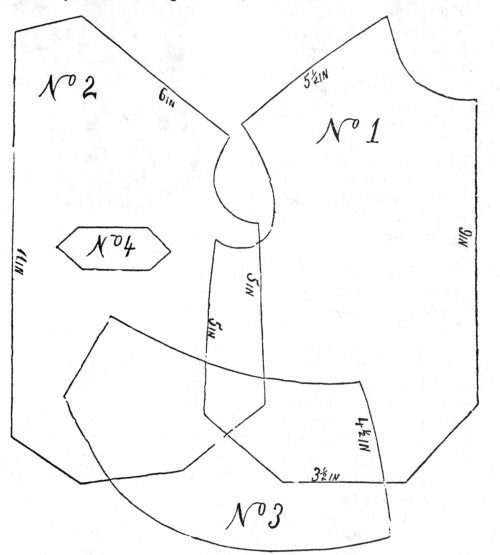

Shirts

Shirts

There is an interesting variety of shirts in the 1860s. The U.S. Army issue was a grey or bluish grey flannel or, in some cases, a knitted wool. Many men found these shirts uncomfortable and wore civilian shirts. As the war wore on and supplies dwindled, this became common practice. The newspapers even ran ads for French flannel army shirts. The civilian shirts they wore reflected those that they would have worn at home and, therefore, reflected their social economic status as a civilian.

Illustrations of the period suggest that many men still wore black pattern shirts made up of squares and rectangles. These were not tailored nor shaped. An illustration of this type of shirt, used for sport in 1869, follows. And probably the best pattern for this type of shirt is from the *Workingwoman's Guide (1837)*. One of these patterns, plus two patterns for civilian shirts and a number of illustrations follow.

Many shirts had detachable collars or cuffs. An interesting ad from around 1863 shows a 'metallic collar' which is actually a good guide to the typical collar of the times. These were much lower than those of the 1850s.

A pattern for a cravat, as well as a knitted neck-tye, can be found in the *Accessories* section.

ads *Harper's Weekly* early 1860s

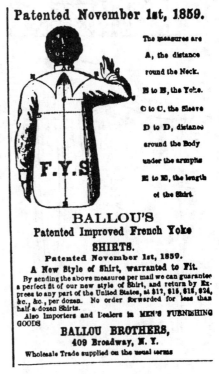

GENERAL RULES FOR CUTTING OUT.

"Waste not, want not."
"Cut your coat according to your cloth."

squares & rectangles shirt
Workingwoman's Guide 1837

measured by cloth measure.

2¼ inches make 1 nail.
4 nails — 1 quarter.
4 quarters — 1 yard.
5 — — 1 English ell.
6 — — 1 French ell.

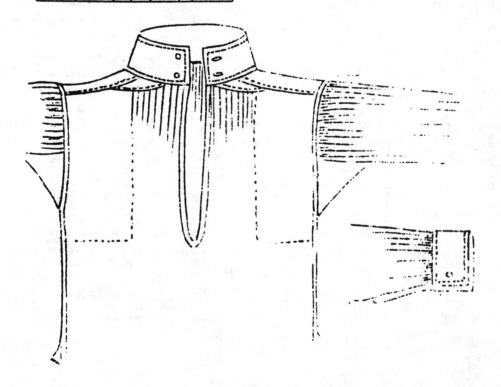

	Fig. 9, Man's larger size.
	Yds. nls.
Quantity required for one	3..8
Quantity required for six.........	21..1
Proper width of cloth	14
Whole length of skirt	2..4
Space to leave for shoulders......	2¼
The space for the neck will then be	9
Slit downwards for bosom	5
Length of arm-holes...............	5¼
Slit at the bottom for flaps	5.
Width of sleeve	8
Length down the selvage..........	8
Width of binders or linings......	3
Length down the selvage..........	12
Width of collar	3
Length down the selvage..........	8
Width of wristband...............	2¼
Length down the selvage..........	4
Width of shoulder-strap	1¼
Length down the selvage..........	4
Size of sleeve-gussets	3
Size of neck-gussets...............	2
Size of bosom-gussets	½
Size of flap-gussets	1

A FEW GENERAL OBSERVATIONS ON SHIRTS.

There are nineteen useful parts to a shirt, which are cut out pretty nearly by the following rough proportions; but as the figures of men differ materially, no exact rule can be laid down.

    1st. The SKIRT OR BODY, which is cut, with the two breadths in one piece, and should be long enough to reach from the shoulder to the knee of the wearer.

    2nd and 3rd. The SLEEVES, which are generally about half the length of the skirt when sewed up, and the breadth the same.

    4th. The COLLAR, which is the same length as the sleeve.

    5th and 6th. The WRISTBANDS, each of which is half the length of the collar.

    7th and 8th. The BINDERS, the length of a sleeve and a quarter.

    9th and 10th. The SHOULDER-STRAPS, the same length as the wristbands.

    11th and 12th. Two SLEEVE-GUSSETS.

    13th and 14th. Two NECK-GUSSETS.

    15th and 16th. Two HIP, or SIDE-GUSSETS.

    17th and 18th. Two WRIST-GUSSETS.

    19th. One BOSOM-GUSSET.

EXPLANATION OF MAKING UP SHIRTS.

Double the long piece for the skirt in two, making the front breadth one nail shorter than the back breadth.

Measure the proper distance from the top for the arm-holes, and the proper distance from the bottom for flaps, and put in pins for marks.

The skirt is usually simply sewed up, but it is preferable, especially with gentlemen's shirts, to make a hem the whole length of the skirt, on each side, and then sew up between the arm-holes and flaps, firmly, with thick even stitches.

Proceed next to stitch the collar and wristbands. Let the stitching be made about six threads from the edge, and carried all round both the wristbands and collar; taking care not to pass the stitches through both folds of them, at the opening or part, in which the fulness of the sleeve or shirt is to be gathered.

Next prepare the straps by turning them in, and drawing the threads; do the same with the neck and other gussets.

Now sew up the sleeves, putting in the large gussets, the little wrist-gussets and gathering them into the wristbands, to prepare them for putting into the shirts. Then put in the side-gussets, and hem the flaps and bottom of the shirt. These gussets are fixed by sewing them on at the wrong side of the shirt to within a quarter of an inch less than the square, and felling the other side nearly over. The neck gussets are next managed in the same manner, taking care to put the stitched part on the right side.

The shoulder-strap is then doubled in half, and slightly tacked on the middle of the shoulder in the inside; then place each side flat on the shirt, and stitch it in the lines that have been prepared for it.

The bosom is then stitched; and the button-holes made, or if, as in gentlemen's shirts, a piece is let into the front, it must be arranged according to the taste of the wearer.

The lining is now neatly felled on, and the neck gathered, and set into the collar, after which the sleeves are gathered and put in. The bosom-bit may then be sewed in, and when the buttons are put on the whole is completed.

The shirt is marked about an inch below the left hip or gusset.

squares & rectangles shirt
Workingwoman's Guide 1837

squares & rectangles shirt
West End Gazette 1869

Shirt, collarless, worn by Gen. David A. Weisiger when wounded at the Battle of the Crater.

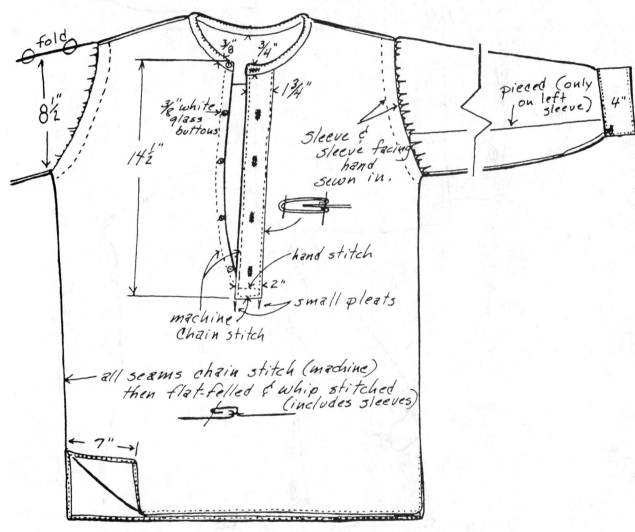

fold

8½"

3/8"

3/4"

3/8" white glass buttons

14½"

1¾"

sleeve & sleeve facing hand sewn in.

pieced (only on left sleeve)

4"

hand stitch

2"

small pleats

machine chain stitch

— all seams chain stitch (machine) then flat-felled & whip stitched (includes sleeves)

7"

Museum of the Confederacy

Confederate general's shirt
reproduced courtesy of Amazon Drygoods
2218 E. 11th St., Davenport, IA 52803

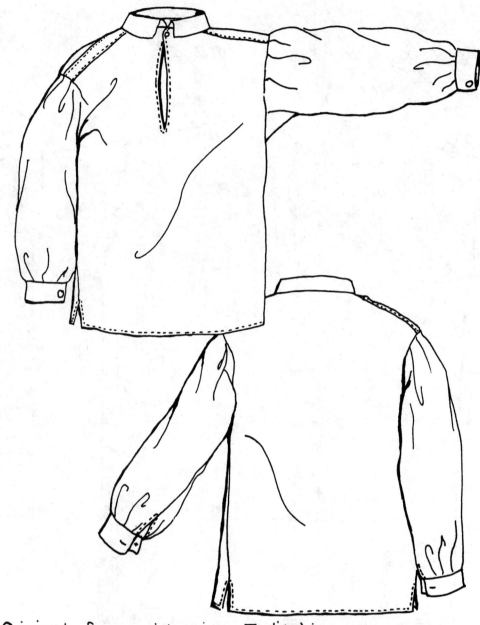

Original from Smithsonian Institution

Union army fatigue shirt
reproduced courtesy of Amazon Drygoods
2218 E. 11th St., Davenport, IA 52803

STYLES AND PRICES OF SHIRTS.
THE FOLLOWING STYLES MADE TO MEASURE.

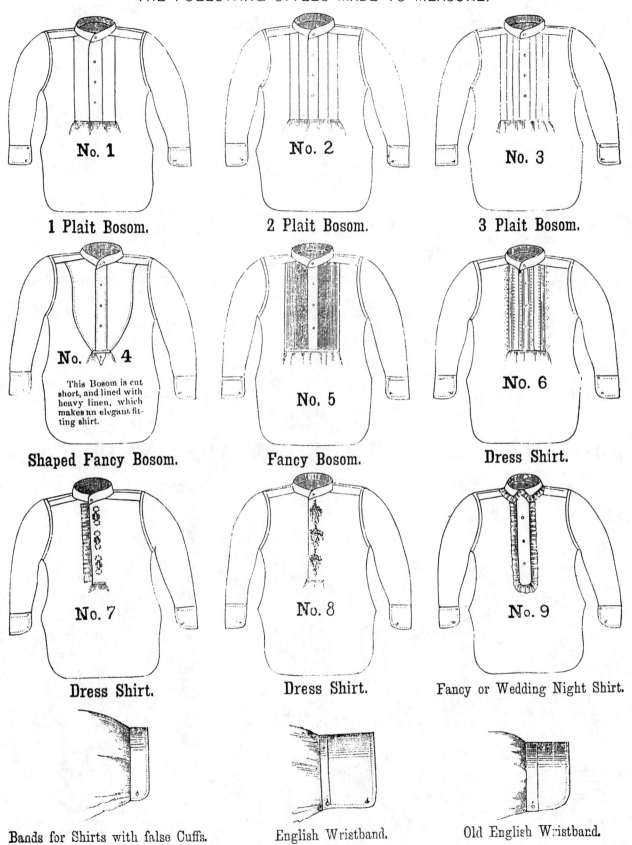

No. 1

1 Plait Bosom.

No. 2

2 Plait Bosom.

No. 3

3 Plait Bosom.

No. 4

This Bosom is cut short, and lined with heavy linen, which makes an elegant fitting shirt.

Shaped Fancy Bosom.

No. 5

Fancy Bosom.

No. 6

Dress Shirt.

No. 7

Dress Shirt.

No. 8

Dress Shirt.

No. 9

Fancy or Wedding Night Shirt.

Bands for Shirts with false Cuffs.

English Wristband.

Old English Wristband.

Ward Shirt & Collar Manufacturing, NY   early 1860s

GENTS' LINEN COLLARS AND CUFFS.

The Dickens.

The Byron.

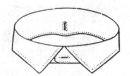
The Young France.

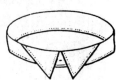
The Piccadilly.

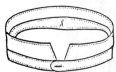
The Guard.

The Stanley.

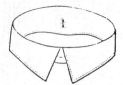
The Shakspeare.

The Narrow Standing.

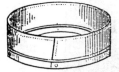
C Standing.

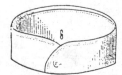
B Standing.

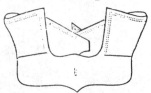
String Linen Collar.

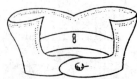
Button Linen Collar.

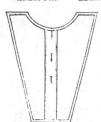
Gents' Reversible Cuffs.

Gents' False Bosoms.

Gents' English Cuffs.

LADIES' AND GENTS' PAPER COLLARS AND CUFFS.

Gents' Argosy Cloth Bosoms.
Paper lined.

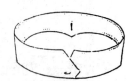
Gents' Reversible Argosy
Cloth Cuffs. Paper lined.

The Dickens Argosy Cloth Collar.
Paper lined.

The Young France Argosy
Linen Collar. Paper lined.

Gents' Argosy Cloth Bosoms.

The Piccadilly Argosy Cloth Collar.
Paper lined.

Gents' French Standing
Argosy Collar. Paper lined.

Ladies' Argosy Turnover Collar.
Paper lined.

The Lady Washington
Cloth lined.

Ladies' English
Tucked Collar.

Ladies' Reversible Paper Cuffs.
Cloth lined.

Ward Shirt & Collar Manufacturing, NY early 1860s

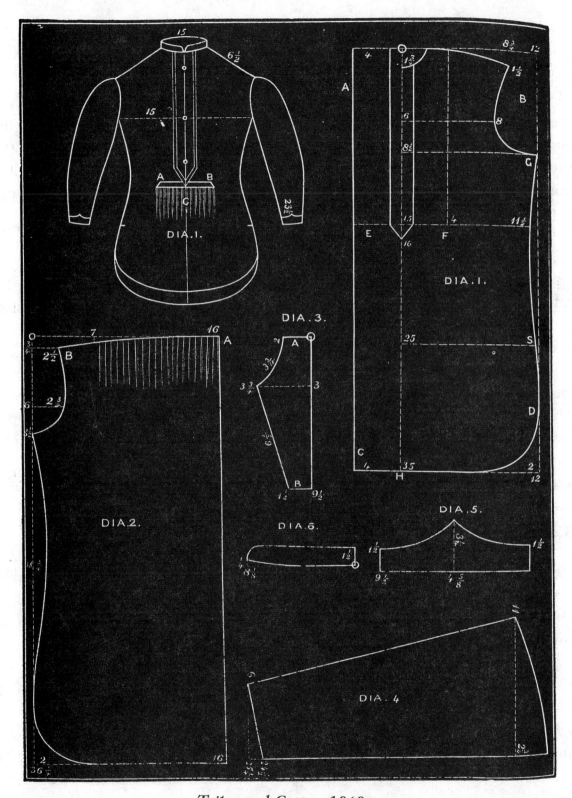

Tailor and Cutter 1868

Shirt Pattern
Tailor and Cutter 1868

In the present issue we are enabled, through the kindness of a friend, to give graduated diagrams of a neat, and very comfortable-fitting shirt; we thought the diagrams would be more useful to our general readers than a complicated divisional system. The quantities given when marked out by the inch tape will produce the shirt for a person measuring 15 neck, 6 1/2 width of shoulder, 23 1/2 length of sleeve, 15 across the chest, wrist 7 1/2, and 36 inches round the breast.

The Front - Diagram 1

Is supposed to be cut out from cotton, or other material 32 inches wide, as represented by the parallel lines A, B, C, D; the side A, C, is the crease or double edge; mark in from A 4 inches for fullness, and draw the construction line O, H; mark down on this line 1 3/4, 6, 8 1/2, 15, 25, 35; mark across 2 1/2, 4, 8 3/4, 12; the shoulder point is lowered 1 1/2 from the 8 3/4; from 6 go across 8 for the front of arm-hole, or half-an-inch more than half the cross chest measure; from 15, 4, and 11 1/2, the sides are left open from the line 25 down, as from S to 12; form the arm-hole from 1 1/2 through 8 to G, and hollow the sides from G to S. Now split the material from the angle at A down to E, and cut it across from E to F. The double edge from E to C is to form the centre of front from 15 to H, and the 4 inches plaited between 15 to F; we generally see one large plait put in the centre at C fig.1, but we much prefer the fullness sent more toward A and B.

The Back - Diagram 2

Has the same quantity of cloth in width as the front, namely 16 inches; the double edge is that from A to 16; draw a square line from O, and mark down 3/4, 6, 8 1/2, 16, 36 1/4, and across 7, 2 1/2, 2 3/4, 3/4, for the hollow of side; from the point to 7 is to be left plain, and the space between 7 and 16 to be gathered to the

Shoulder Piece - Diagram 3

which is to be drawn out by the quantities shown on the diagram, starting at O to 3 and 9 1/2, the width across the shoulders, to which the back in A B is to be gathered; end A - 2 wide is te (sic) middle, and to be placed at A, dia. 2 from 2 to 3 1/4 in the back neck; 3 3/4 to 1 1/2 the shoulder-seam, to be sewed to that of dia. 1 from 2 1/2 to 1 1/2, with end B, which is 1 1/2 wide place at B, dia. 2.

The Sleeve - Diagram 4

Is cut from cotton 36 inches wide, and 26 inches long, taken out, "one up and one down." The line on which is marked 2 3/4, 24 1/2, and 25 1/4 is the double edge, but may be made with or without a seam; 11 and 6 are the widths at top and bottom, the latter to be plaited or held full to the

Wristband - Diagram 5

Which is made 9 1/2 inches in length, to allow for making-up, 1 1/2 wide at the ends, and 3 1/4 at the point. In the absence of measure the wrist is generally made half the circumference of the neck 15, wrist 7 1/2, or the neck made twice the size of wrist. There are various other relative proportions which are useful as guides when cutting stock garments of this kind.

The Collar - Diagram 6

Is cut two inches longer than the real size of the neck, this is the necessary allowance for making-up and button-stand; the sewing on edge is rounded half-an-inch from a straight line, one inch deep in front, and one and a-half deep behind.

Tailor and Cutter 1868

squares & rectangles shirt
'The Boys of 61'

Norfolk Shirt or Blouse.

TO THE EDITOR OF THE WEST-END GAZETTE.

DEAR SIR,—As several correspondents have asked for a pattern of a Norfolk Shirt or Blouse, I have sent you one for publication. It will be seen at a glance that it is cut similar to a lounge jacket, but has, in addition, a box plait laid on each forepart, and one down the centre of back. The plaits are shown by the roulette lines. It has a stand collar, four holes up the front, two breast pockets put in lengthways, and is fastened at the waist by a belt made of the same material. The sleeves are plaited in at the wrist, as I have marked them, and I leave a slit of about three inches, and put a hole and button in the wristband.

It forms a very becoming garment for young gentlemen when made either in unbleached brown Holland, Alpaca, or Tweed, in which case the plaits should be sewn down.

Faithfully yours,

M—K W—N.

West End Gazette 1866

pattern following page

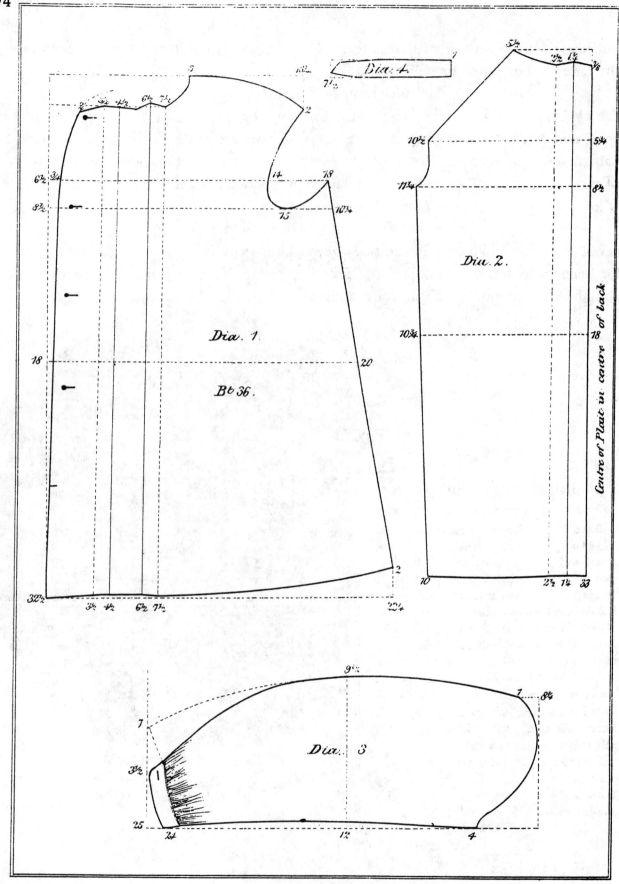

Norfolk Shirt
West End Gazette 1866

Accessories

Accessories

Some of the things men wore when they were more relaxed were really very colorful. These articles are often made by women at home and reflect a great deal of love and caring. They also often reflected the influence of Turkey and the Orient on fashion. A number of these follow from *Civil War Ladies*. As smoking became popular, so to did smoking accessories. A further selection of smoking caps and slippers can be found in Hartley's *The Ladies' Hand Book of Fancy & Ornamental Work*.

There is a cravat pattern from <u>Harper's Bazar</u>, March 13, 1869, and a pattern for gaiters from Devere's <u>Gentleman's Magazine</u>, 1869. Other patterns for gaiters (which were used by both civilians and the military) can be found in Devere's *The Hand Book of Practical Cutting on the Centre Point System* (p. 61), and Minister's *The Complete Guide to Practical Cutting* (p. 164).

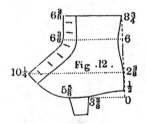

Gaiters

Fig. 12 is the pattern of a short gaiter, to be made in waterproofed cloth, and worn for shooting, or with the proposed Rifle Costume

Devere's *Gentlemen's Magazine* 1859

SMOKING-CAP IN APPLICATION.

BY MRS. JANE WEAVER.

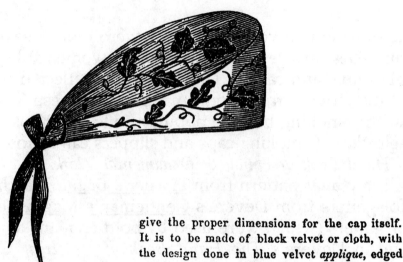

give the proper dimensions for the cap itself. It is to be made of black velvet or cloth, with the design done in blue velvet *applique*, edged with white silk or gold embroidery braid, **as the**

WE give, here, a pretty design for a Smoking-Cap in application of what is called the Scotch shape. In the diagram, accompanying this, we taste may suggest. Line the cap with black silk, wadded and quilted. Finish with a bow of narrow black ribbon at the back.

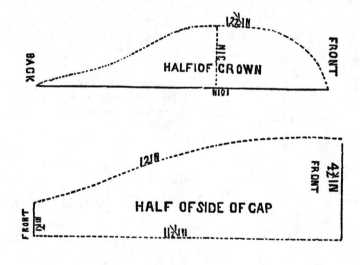

Peterson's Magazine 1864

IMPERIAL LOUNGING-CAP.

BY MRS. JANE WEAVER.

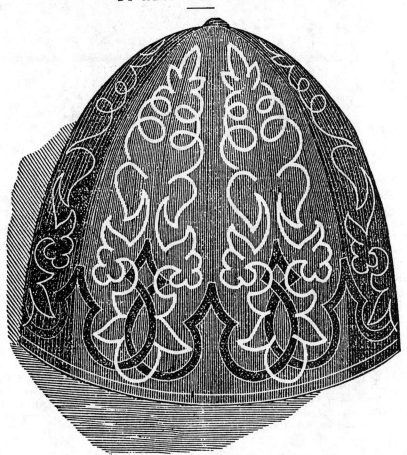

THE Imperial Lounging-Cap possesses a very Oriental appearance when seen complete. It is composed of six portions of velvet in two alternate colors, a rich violet and dark crimson. The scroll, which appears black in the illustration, is formed of narrow black ribbon velvet, with a gold thread at each edge. The design may be braided in narrow gold braid, or two silk braids of different colors. A violet braid on the crimson velvet, and a crimson braid on the violet velvet, has a very rich effect. A long silk tassel made of the two colors, interspersed with gold, is fastened at the top, and hangs down the side of the cap. This would make a very pretty Christmas, New-Year's, or birthday gift for a gentleman.

Peterson's Magazine 1864

BRAIDED SEGAR–CASE.

BY MRS. JANE WEAVER.

THE materials are cloth, velvet, braid, and steel beads. Take a sufficient quantity of fine cashmere, of any suitable color, and carefully sew on a piece of black or dark velvet, shaped as in the pattern. Then transfer the pattern. This may be easily done by carefully drawing it with chalk on a piece of paper, and pressing the paper evenly on the cloth and velvet, or by tracing the pattern well with cotton. Then sew on the braid in the usual manner, and attach the beads. Repeat the process for the other side of the Segar-Case, and fasten together the two sides to form the outer envelope. The inner case may be made of silk or satin, neatly stitched over card-board. Finish the edges of the outer case with cord or braid, and when the one case is placed inside the other, a very pretty and even elegant piece of work will have been produced. It is important that the inner case be made to fit accurately into the outer one. A small loop of narrow ribbon is to be attached to the upper end of the inner case. On one side of the outer case the initials or name of the recipient may be formed, with steel or gold beads, on the center-piece of velvet. This Segar-Case is very beautiful.

BRAIDING PATTERN.

Peterson's Magazine 1865

GENTLEMAN'S NECK-TYE IN BRIOCHE KNITTING.

BY MRS. JANE WEAVER.

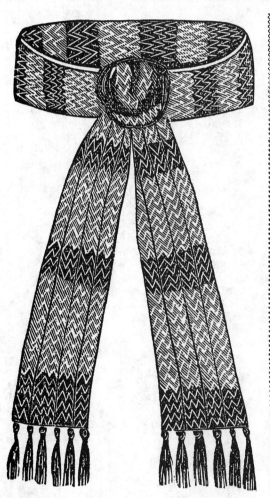

skeins of magenta, mauve or claret, double Berlin wool; a pair of knitting-needles No. 3.

Commence with the black wool, cast on twenty-six stitches.

1st Row.—Black, bring the wool in front of the needle, slip the first stitch, then knit the next stitch plain; continue to bring the wool forward, slip one and knit one to the end of the row. This row forms the foundation and is not to be repeated.

2nd Row.—Bring the wool in front, slip one, then knit the two stitches which cross together; repeat to the end. All the rows are now the same.

Work three rows more as the second row, still using the black wool; join on the partridge wool. Every two rows form one link or chain in depth.

Work four rows with the partridge wool, then ten rows the same, using the magenta or mauve wool. Work four rows with the partridge wool. These four stripes form one pattern.

Commence again with the black, work six rows as before, and then repeat the partridge and magenta stripes until the required length is made. Cast off.

THE FRINGE.—Cut the magenta and partridge wools in lengths of eight inches, take three of these pieces, and with a crochet needle loop them into a link of the knitting, bringing the ends through the loop and then drawing them tight. Continue the same along both ends.

We recommend this for a present for the holidays.

MATERIALS.—Two skeins of black; three skeins of brown and white partridge, and three

If a boot is not desired, a slipper can be made, taking the slipper-part for the pattern, supersede the slipper, as many gentlemen catch cold by changing from a boot to a slipper, even

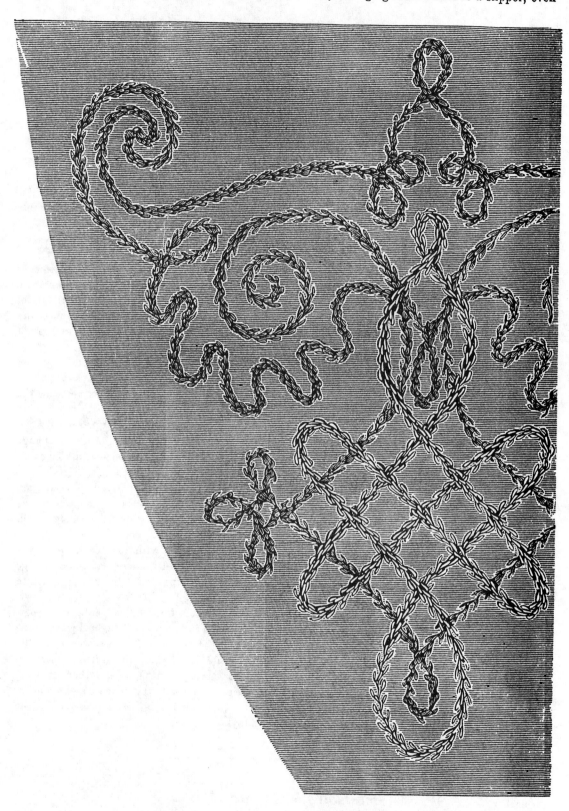

which will be found of a size adapted to the foot of most gentlemen.

The Lounging Boot, however, will almost

in the house. The novelty of the Lounging Boot, too, will increase its popularity; and it is easily worked.

GENTLEMAN'S BRACES.

BY MRS. JANE WEAVER.

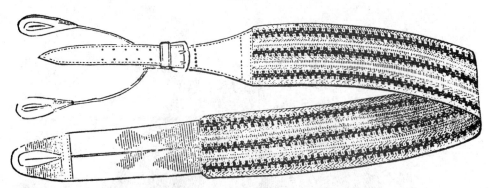

MATERIALS.—10 skeins of cerise, and 5 each of black and maize crochet silk. Make a chain 150 stitches with the cerise. 1st row: Work a stitch of double crochet, make a chain, miss 1 loop, repeat. 2nd row: Turn, make 1 chain, work a stitch of double crochet into the chain of last row, make 1 chain, repeat. Every row is alike. Work 2 rows of cerise, 2 of black, 2 of cerise, 2 of maize, 2 of cerise, 2 of black, 2 of cerise, 2 of maize, 2 of cerise, 2 of black, and 2 of cerise; this completes the brace. The crochet should not be done too tightly, as a little elasticity is desirable. When finished, the lengths left at the end of the rows must be neatly run in, and some kid brace ends, that are kept ready for the purpose, stitched on. No lining is required, both sides of the work being exactly alike.

Peterson's Magazine **1864**

GENTLEMAN'S DRESSING OR LOUNGING BOOT.

BY MRS. JANE WEAVER.

BEFORE commencing to work this boot, which is warm, comfortable, more elegant than a slipper, and much newer in style, the proper measures should be taken by a shoemaker, who should be told the dimensions the boot should be, so as to leave sufficient space, free of embroidery, for making it up.

Our pattern is made of brown cloth, embroidered in two shades of brown silk, lighter than the cloth. Both shades are clearly marked in the separate illustration we give of the full-size pattern on the upper part of the foot (for which see next page): the same pattern is repeated on the leg.

This pattern may be worked either in herring-bone, in chain stitch, or braiding. In the two last cases, a double row should be worked; these rows may be either of two different colors, or, if preferred, of two distinct shades of the same color.

Peterson's Magazine **1864**

TOBACCO-BAG.

BY MRS. JANE WEAVER.

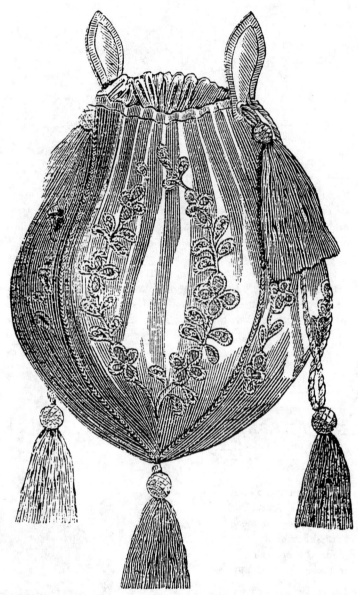

THIS bag may be made of velvet, silk, cloth, or cashmere. The section is one-fourth of the bag in its full size. The flowers and leaves are in application edged with braid, and the leaves are dotted with beads.

Braid may be put on to cover each seam of the sections; one of which (full-size) is given in the front of the number.

The bag is usually lined with wash-leather or kid, and rings are sewn inside to pass the cord through. Small silk cord and tassels are used, or gold, if preferred. A very pretty bag may be made with a scarlet cloth, black velvet application, gold beads, braid, cord, and tassels. This is a very suitable birthday gift to a gentleman.

SMOKING-CAP.

BY MRS. JANE WEAVER.

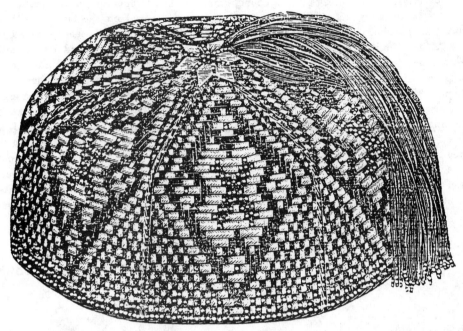

MATERIALS.—Fifty yards of black double braid; twenty-five yards of blue braid; two yards and a half of black single braid; one skein of black silk cordon: one bunch of steel beads, No. 5; twenty-nine inches of black sarsnet ribbon, two inches and a half broad; a stiff

The cap, represented in the design, consists of six parts, four inches broad and six inches high. Each part must be worked separately in a little wooden or strong wire frame. The inside of the frame must be six inches and a half high and five inches broad.

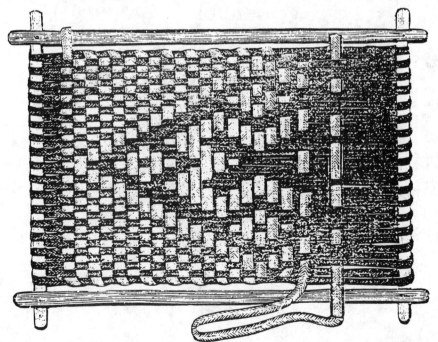

piece of cardboard, two and a half inches square; a piece of blue sarsnet, two and a half inches square.

No. 2 shows the frame, and the mode of working the braid, in a reduced size.

Fasten the black double braid to one of the

cross-bars; wind them from the under part upward seventeen times evenly, close to each other, so that there will be thirty-three braids, and then sew the end to the beginning over in a slanting direction. Slip a piece of whalebone, rather longer than the width of the frame, into the blue braid; make a hole in it at each end, and sew the braid to it. This forms the needle. As in common darning, one stitch is worked over and one under, alternately, until the pattern begins, which is clearly shown in No. 2.

The under broad part continues for the first sixteen rows. In the eight following, the edges are sloped off one stitch in each row of the lace, and then two as far as the point.

Before the work is taken out of the frame, the braids of the outer plaited row must be securely fastened together with stitches of black sewing-silk, and ornamented with steel beads, according to No. 1. Afterward, the ends are laid inside and firmly sewn together at the sides and under edge. The separate plaited parts of the cap must be sewn together on the wrong side, and the seam covered on the outside with a braid border, and dotted with steel beads. The points are firmly fastened to a round piece of silk, hemmed on the wrong side. The under edge of the cap is lined with black sarsnet ribbon, and bound with braid. For the outer edge, a black silk cordon tassel, eight inches long, hangs down from the upper middle, ornamented at each double end with three steel beads. In the middle is a button in the shape of a star, cut out of cardboard, and covered with blue sarsnet. Each of the divisions of the star is ornamented with silk cordon, braid, and beads. (See design.)

TOBACCO-POUCH.

BY MRS. JANE WEAVER.

WE give, in the front of the number, a design, printed in colors, for a Tobacco-Pouch: a very suitable present from a lady to a gentleman. We also give one section, full size, with the proper embroidery and braiding pattern on it. The bag should be made of red kid, such as is used for topping ladies' boots, and may easily be procured at the shoemaker's. Embroider with fine black silk the initials of the person for whom it is designed; also the Turk. Do the dress in the silk, and the face and hands indicate by fine strokes of a pen, or camel's-hair brush and India ink; the braiding is of black silk braid. Six sections compose the pouch, all of which should be braided, using the same, or different patterns for every section; of course, omitting the Turk and initials after the first one. Finish with a tassel at the bottom, and cords to draw at the top, which are passed through eyelets, either worked or such as are put in boots. These pretty affairs are very desirable for sea-shore and country.

TOBACCO POUCH

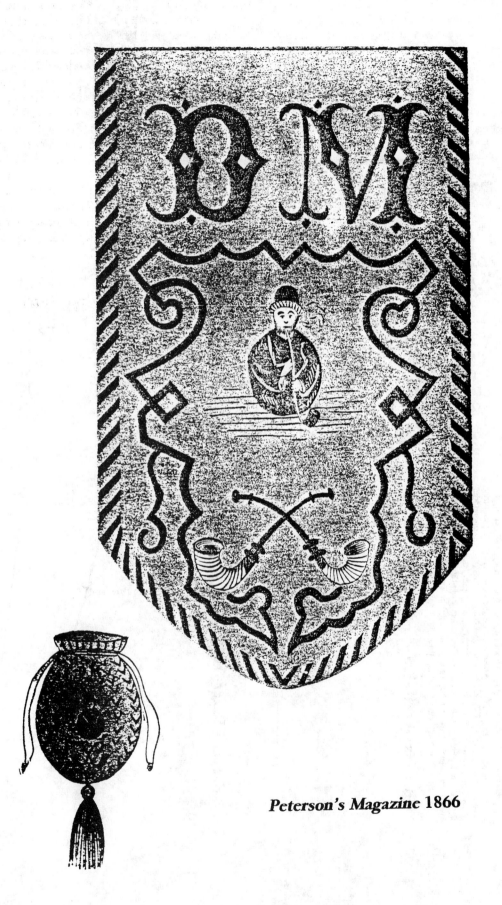

Peterson's Magazine 1866

Pattern for a cravat - mistitled a 'stock' because it is permanently tied and fastened with a buckle. A stock is a form of collar/tie combination.

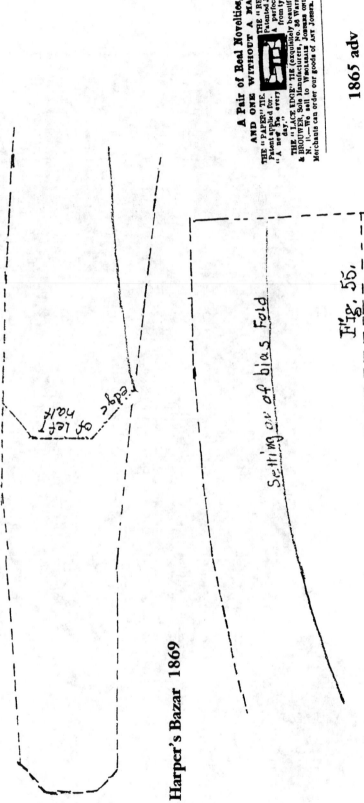

No. XVI. Gentleman's Stock.   See Illustration.

Gentleman's Stock.

Fig. 55. Half of Stock.

This stock or neckerchief is of black silk reps, and is fastened with a buckle be-hind. It may also be made of satin, gros grain, etc. Cut from Fig. 55 one piece; but cut the left half only as far as the dotted line on Fig. 55. Line with stiff muslin and silk and sew the edges together with a cord. Set a bias piece of silk along the straight line on Fig. 55, letting it extend over on the wrong side. The material must stand up loosely by the seam so as to imitate another binding. On the middle of the front fasten a little bow, the ends of which are pointed. On the shortest end of the stock fasten a buckle of suitable size, and on the other side under the front end a long piece for fastening. The end of the right half of the stock comes over the buckle and covers it, and is then put through a narrow band of the material.

("Rep" is ribbed silk)

Harper's Bazar 1869

Fig. 55.

edge of left half

Setting on of bias. Fold

Civil War Uniforms

Notes on Civil War Uniforms
And the Search for Patterns

Uniforms during the Civil War were not dull and drab, they were not straight forward, they often times did not follow the regulations, and they certainly were not, for the most part, the simplistic things represented in romantic paintings and some movies and television.

In the beginning of the war, which most people thought would be short, the armies resembled something out of a European Operetta. Although there was uniformity in the 'army' of each side, there were also the volunteers from each state in their own particular dress (often outfitted by a patron to his liking), the various state militia and National Guard, and various special units like those formed by various newly arrived immigrants (especially in New York city). The uniforms ranged from the kilt, to a number of different Zoauve outfits (the Louisiana Zouaves wore stripped trousers and were called the 'Tigers', their uniforms were paid for by the businessmen of New Orleans), to Garibaldi outfits, quasi English uniforms, Hussar outfits, straw boaters worn by some of the Confederate Navy, fancy shakos, etc. The 3rd New Jersey Calvary's (or '1st U.S. Hussars', as they preferred to be known)` uniforms were so fancy that they were called 'butterflies' by the other troops. Whatever else you might say about Civil War uniforms, they definitely were not all either blue or grey.

As the war progressed there were attempts at uniformity on some levels, and at other levels diversity was encouraged. The frock coat was supposed to be standard for both sides, but it was not very practical for active service and was replaced by the sack coat. Also as supplies dwindled the armies mixed their clothing with civilian items and whatever else they could find.

The South had particular problems because although they had cotton, they did not have mills and so had trouble procuring cloth. This led to clothing made of homespun (wool and cotton mixed and woven at home). Reportedly this cloth was dyed with a mixture of nutshells and iron filings producing a 'butternut' color. Many of the Confederate soldiers also took articles of clothing from dead Union soldiers and prisoners of war (causing the prisoners undue hardship from the cold). This became so prevalent that at one point the Union threatened to shoot as spies any enemy troops wearing articles of Union clothing. And of course they, like the Union soldiers, often got replacements for worn out clothing from home. It has been said that "Towards the end of the war, as a result of the shortage of supplies in the South, the sight of an even approximately correctly uniformed infantryman was very unusual".

On the other side there were a number of Union outfits that had grey uniforms (for example the Pennsylvania Reserves) which they wouldn't even consider giving up. They were often killed by 'friendly fire'. Many units learned to discard some of their brighter and more flashy items of clothing (and often insignia) so that they would not be picked off by snipers. The "Union blue' color also was not standard and ranged from a light blue to almost black. And again, worn out uniforms would often be replaced with articles from home.

Both the Union and the Confederacy bought uniforms in Europe. This was true for Zouave type uniforms, and the Union also managed to buy 10,000 chasseur uniforms from France. The jackets of these had a small skirt which can be seen in the sketch in the *7th Regiment* Section. This is one of those cases where the government itself was perpetuating differences from the Dress Regulations.

Also it must be remembered that there is a vast difference between formal posed portrait photographs, where people wore parade style uniforms, and those uniforms you see in the more candid photos and drawings - let alone what was worn in actual battle.

It is said that Grant judged a man by the way he fought not the state of his uniform. And indeed Grant, judging by the photographs of him, was fairly sloppy and liked to wear his collar down in civilian style, as did many other officers. It is also said that Lee "always wore during the campaign a gray sack coat with side pockets like the costume of a business man in the cities".

The basic reason why no one has written the definitive manual for Civil War uniforms from a tailoring standpoint is that there really are no surviving patterns (one exception being a Confederate frock coat pattern which will follow). Added to this is the question of "what would you present if you could?". The Dress Regulations are all well and good but they only represent a part of the story. Both armies based their uniforms on the 1855 regulations. These were revised in 1861 by both the Union and the Confederacy, but remained very similar to each other. Whether they liked it or not the two armies grew from a single ancestor. General Lee went through West Point, fought in the Mexican War and was Superintendent of West Point between 1852 and 1855. Also, Jefferson Davis graduated from West Point and was Secretary of War in the U.S. government before the war.

Bearing in mind that there is very little that can be presented in the way of patterns for uniforms on either side, there are some possibilities that can be used. This depends upon which of the many uniforms is to be produced and how good the person is at tailoring. In terms of research there are a number of very detailed books listed in the *bibliography* which are well worth using. However, two books that will give a quick overview are Lloyd's *Combat Uniforms of the Civil War* and Katcher's *The American Soldier: U.S. Armies in uniform, 1755 to the present.* The illustrations are in color, but they definitely are not primary source material. Once having decided upon the uniform, it will have to be researched more thoroughly with some of the books that go into more detail. It is at this point that some attempt can be made at finding a tailoring pattern that will be usable (probably with adaptations). In line with this it might be possible to produce some of the more British and Hussar looking uniforms by using either Devere's *The Handbook of Practical Cutting on the Centre Point System* or possibly Minister's *The Complete Guide to Practical Cutting,* both of which have uniform sections in them.

One of the most interesting uniforms used in the Civil War by both the Union and the Confederacy was the Zouave. These were originally Algerian uniforms that were adopted by the French when they took over that country. There is no denying that they are exotic. So much so that they found their way into women's fashions (see *Civil War Ladies* for both illustrations and patterns for Zouave jackets for women) and boys fashions (see Devere's *The Handbook of Practical Cutting on the Centre Point System* p. 71 for a pattern, and illustrations can be found in both the *7th Regiment* section, in the *Additional Illustrations* section of this book and further along in this article). The components of the basic French Zouave uniform are shown here in a drawing by Michael J. McAfee from his exhibit catalog *Zouave: The First and the Bravest* and it is reproduced courtesy of him.

A pattern for gaiters, which would have been worn with Zouave uniforms, can be found in the *Accessories* section.

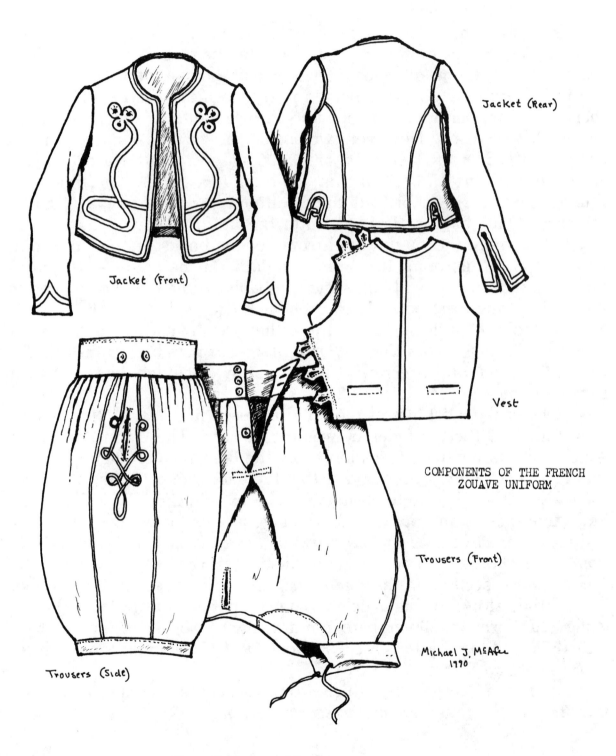

Jacket (Front)

Jacket (Rear)

Vest

COMPONENTS OF THE FRENCH
ZOUAVE UNIFORM

Trousers (Front)

Trousers (Side)

Michael J. McAfee
1970

French Zouave Uniform

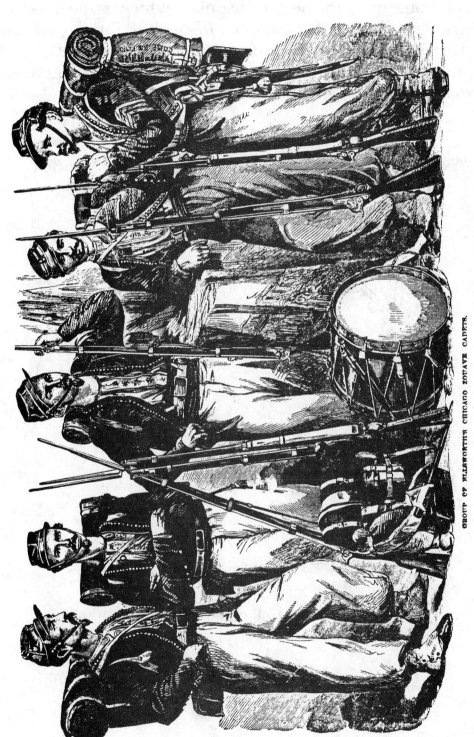

GROUP OF ELLSWORTH'S CHICAGO ZOUAVE CADETS.

Chicago Zouaves

This is an official drawing of a Marine uniform of 1859. Many of these elements did not change. Note that the coat shown is an overcoat. The trousers are particularly interesting when compared with the sketch of the infantry trousers from the Smithsonian which appear later in this article. Schuyler, Hartley & Graham's *Illustrated Catalog of Civil War Military Goods* (which is available as a reprint) gives dress regulations for the Army, Navy and Marines as they existed in 1864. It is interesting to see how well these drawings compare to those regulations.

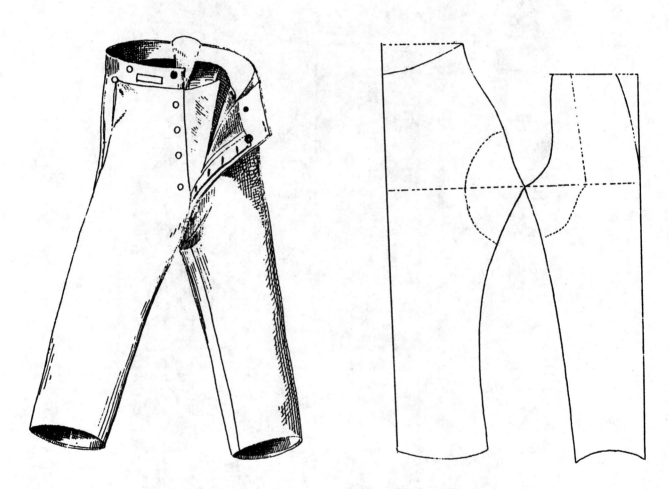

Pattern for cut of enlisted men's Trowsers.

Marine Trousers

Top of Officers Cap
Full size   (Undress)

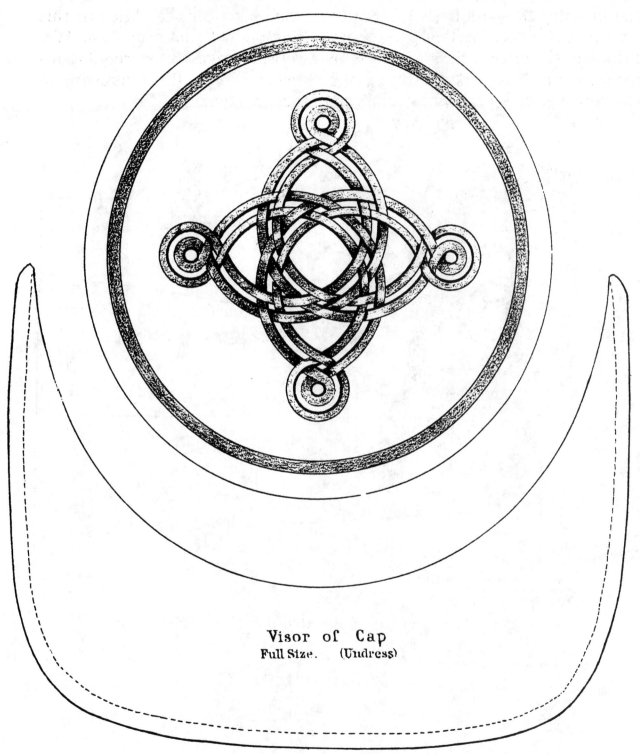

Visor of Cap
Full Size.   (Undress)

Marine Officer's Cap

*Visor to be bound with glazed leather, same as that
of which it is made*

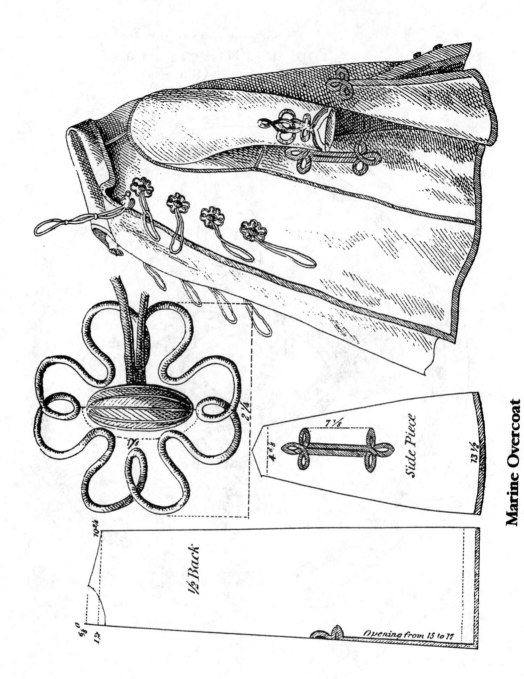

198

Marine Overcoat

Side Piece

7 ⅛

4 ⅜

13 ½

2 ¼

1 ⅞

½ Back

10 ¼

6 0

1 ½

Opening from 15 to 17

Note:
The figures are in inches

This drawing is for a coat for a man 5 ft. 2 in.

Badges of rank,
worn on sleeves of overcoat.

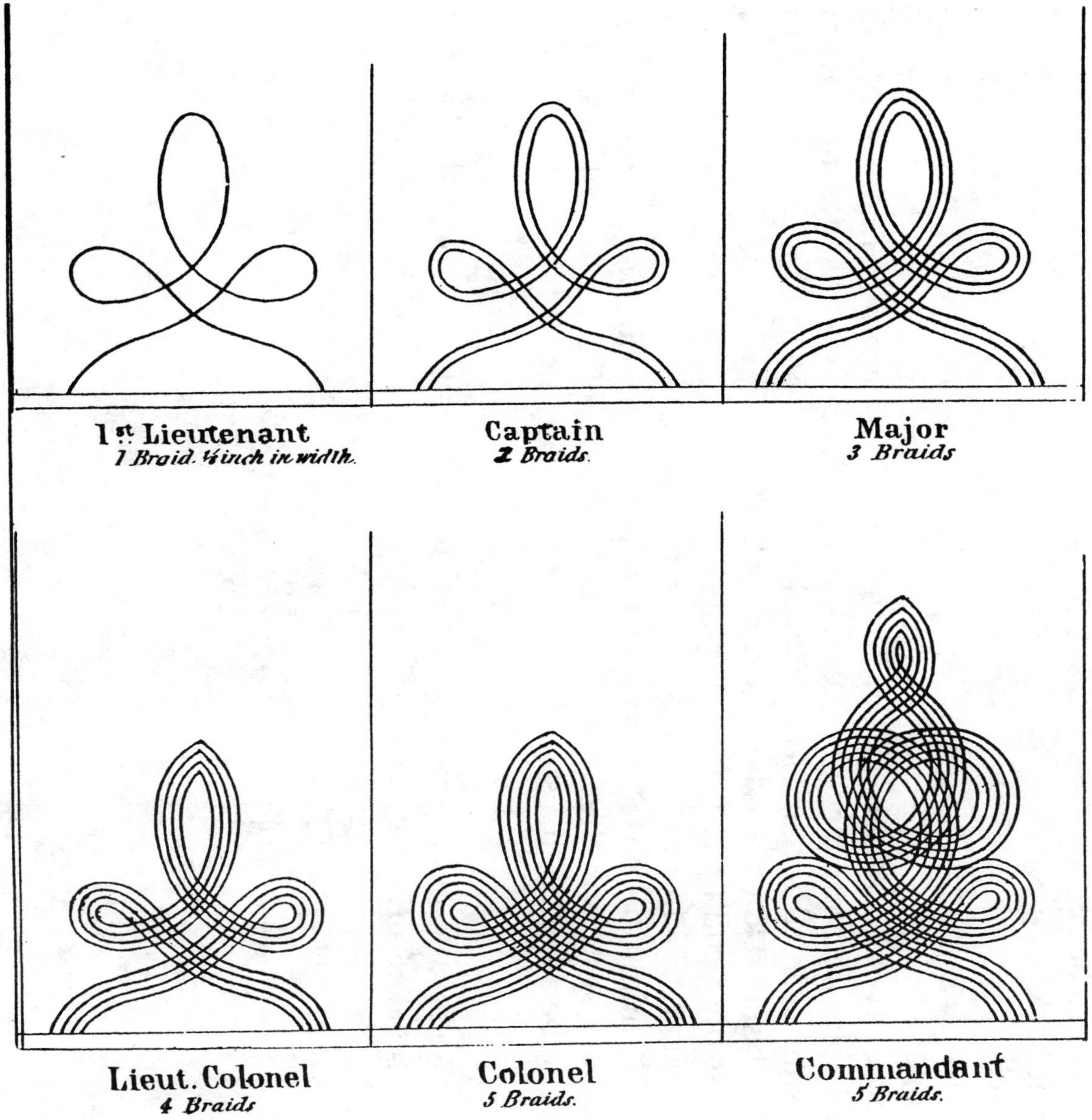

1st Lieutenant
1 Braid. ¼ inch in width.
Captain
2 Braids.
Major
3 Braids
Lieut. Colonel
4 Braids
Colonel
5 Braids.
Commandant
5 Braids.

Front Piece
0 6/8
3 1/8
7 5/8
11 3/8
9 7/8
18 7/8
15
18 1/2
71 2/8
6 6/8

Marine Overcoat

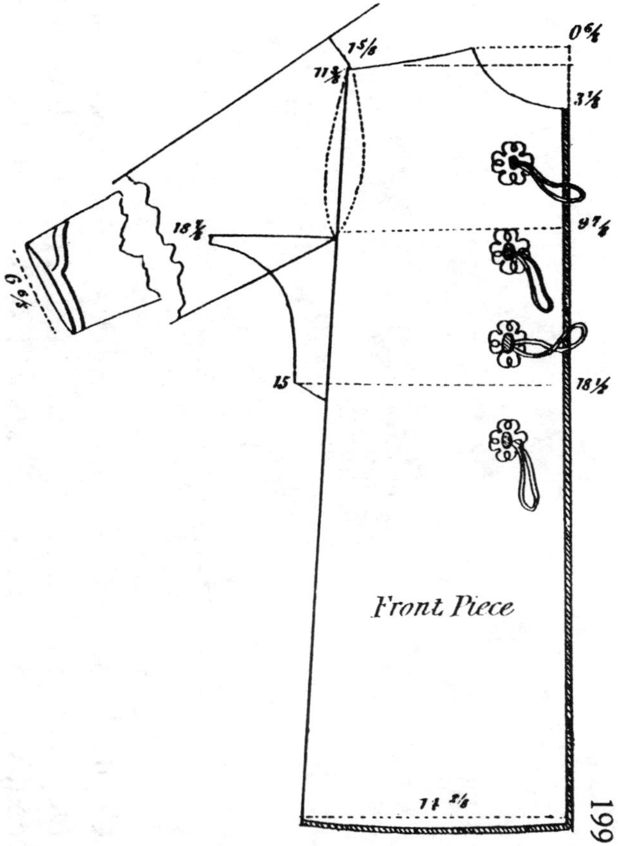

Luckily there is a 'Tailor's Plate' which has survived of a Confederate military frock coat from 1861, approved by the War Department, Richmond, Virginia. This is a double breasted frock military coat with a standing collar. It has been labeled for easier use:

1. sleeve - with a dotted line drawn in to show where the under sleeve would be.
2. front body
3. lapel - to be cut separate and stitched on.
4. side back body
5. back
6. skirt
7. collar
8. possibly a Havelock - a lightweight cloth covering (usually white & washable) for a military cap (kepi), long in back to protect the neck from the sun. Named for Sir Henry Havelock, 19th Century English general in India, but best known as being worn by the French in Africa.
9. possibly a cuff - but if so it is out of scale.
C = center. F = front. B = back.

It might be possible to use the pattern for the frock coat in the Salisbury system in the front of the book (plate #4), but the collar would have to be adapted to a standing collar.

N.B. We have now had a confirmation from the Smithsonian that #8 on the **Tailor's Plate** is indeed a Havelock and #9 is a cuff.

TAILOR'S PLATE

LITH. DRAWING BY E. CREHEN. RICHMOND

APPROVED BY WAR DEPARTMENT

LITH. PRINTING BY VALORY PETERSBURG VA

Confederate Military Frock Coat

The following pattern for a double breasted frock coat from Devere's *Gentleman's Magazine* 1860 comes pretty close to the dress regulations, but the pattern lacks a collar so one would have to be adapted from somewhere else.

Figs. 1, 2, 3, 4 are the patterns of a double-breasted frock-coat or jacket with a seam at waist, presenting, in comparison with our medium type, to that we have adopted as the proportionate, the following differences.

The turnover has a width of 3 1/8 more than the fixed measure, which gives a greater amplitude to the chest, and admits the buttons being placed at a greater distance from the edge. The edge of turnover is cut nearly square, which gives, consequently, too great width at the waist, which must be reduced by taking out a fish in the forepart, between 9 7/8, 10 5/8.

For the side-body, we have, in this diagram, taken out a fish under the arm, instead of springing it out for the swell of the hip, at the same time taking account of the differences, which will consist in giving more depth to the bottom of the back-stretch, instead of the side-point.

It is well known that taking out a fish under the arm lowers the side-point about 3/8 of an inch, consequently in this pattern we have to discover, how and where we have raised this point, for it remains at its usual number, 1 1/2 on the line 7 1/2. It remains there, it is true; but let us see farther, and we shall see the differences is allowed for in the back, because the bottom of back-stretch is at 5 7/8 instead of 5 1/2, as in the regular pattern, so the 3/8 which is taken from the height of side-point by the fish under the arm, is added to the bottom of back-stretch.

From this we conclude that in drafting a forepart we may take out a fish for the hollow of the hip, instead of springing it out at the bottom, but on this condition that we leave 3/8 more at the bottom of back-stretch, because this fish lowers all the back part of the garment, and at the same we must widen the waist at the back, to make up for this same loss, either 3/8 or 3/4 according to the hollow of the hip. Fig. 3 is the skirt, it is of a medium length and fulness.

The sleeve, fig 4, has one seam only, and is wide at the elbow, this style being much worn at the present time; to draft this sleeve, we proceed in the following manner: draft the top side of the tight-filling sleeve in the ordinary manner as shown by the dotted lines; then lengthen these lines square on the other side of the construction line, repeating the numbers to obtain the under side of sleeve, except giving less width to the top of under side (7 1/2 instead of 8 5/8), as the arm is less in this part. After having drafted these two pieces opposite each other, regulate the curves of the top and bottom from the diagram; experience will soon teach the precise quantity to add in order to destroy the angles which exist without these corrections. The pattern thus modified gives the numbers shewn on fig. 4.

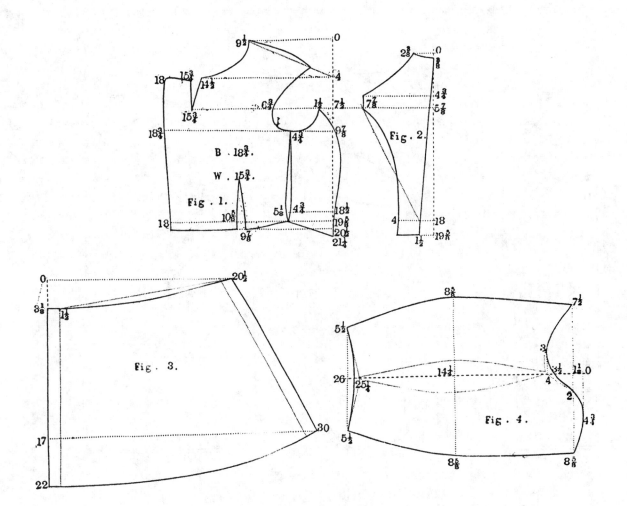

Double Breasted Frock Coat

Again, there is no pattern for a fatigue sack coat but the following one from Minister's *Gazette of Fashion* 1863 comes very close.

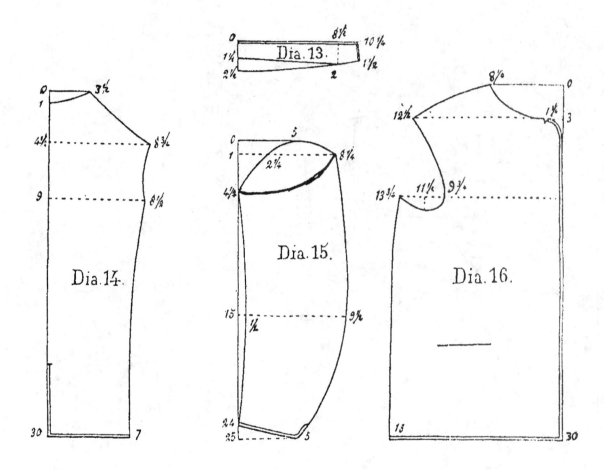

Possible Fatigue Coat

Again there is no pattern for a shell jacket, but these pattern drafts from Devere's *Gentlemen's Magazine* of 1861 could be used with some care and adaptations.

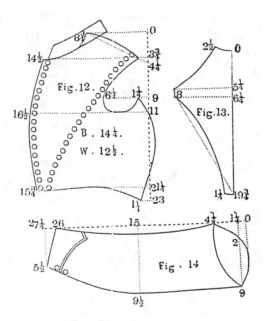

Possible Shell Jacket

Shirts are dealt with in the *Shirts* section of civilian wear because so many men wore civilian shirts rather than the military issue (if indeed they were lucky enough to be issued shirts in the first place). There are sketches of both military and civilian shirts, and patterns for making shirts of the period. There is a pattern for a cravat in the *Accessories* section as they were the same for both military and civilian wear.

Trousers were fairly loose and had to be worn over a boot. Adaptations could be made to the trousers given in the Salisbury system or to those in Devere's *The Handbook of Practical Cutting on the Centre Point System..* In both cases these patterns can be followed as a general rule and 17 inches at the bottom should work well to accommodate the boot. One of the major problems is that they do not have a yoke, nor do they have a belt in the back. The belt is not always common as can be seen in the following sketch of an actual pair of infantry trousers in the Smithsonian. It gives variations for both the pocket and the treatment of the back. This sketch is reproduced courtesy of *Amazon Drygoods, 2218 E. 11th St. Davenport, IA 52803.* It is interesting to compare this sketch with the ones given for the marine uniform which appear earlier in this section.

Infantryman's Trousers

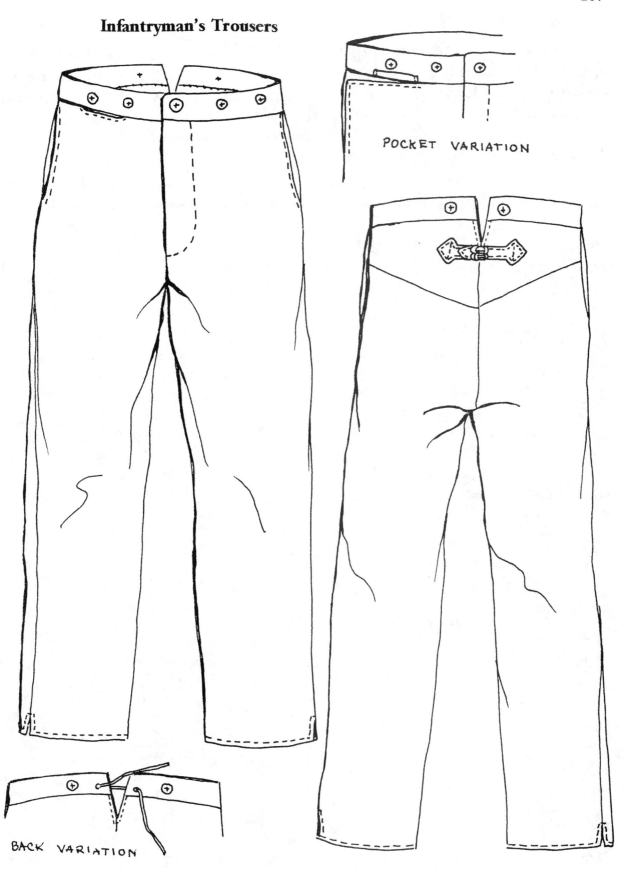

POCKET VARIATION

BACK VARIATION

Original from Smithsonian Institution

Overcoats had standing collars and a cape, see the *1861 Dress Regulations* section. Adaptations would have to be made from an existing coat pattern to meet collar regulations, length of the coat, and length of the cape, etc. The one that seems to be most in the spirit of the dress regulations is this pattern of a military over-coat for the Rifle Corps from Devere's *Gentleman's Magazine* of 1860.

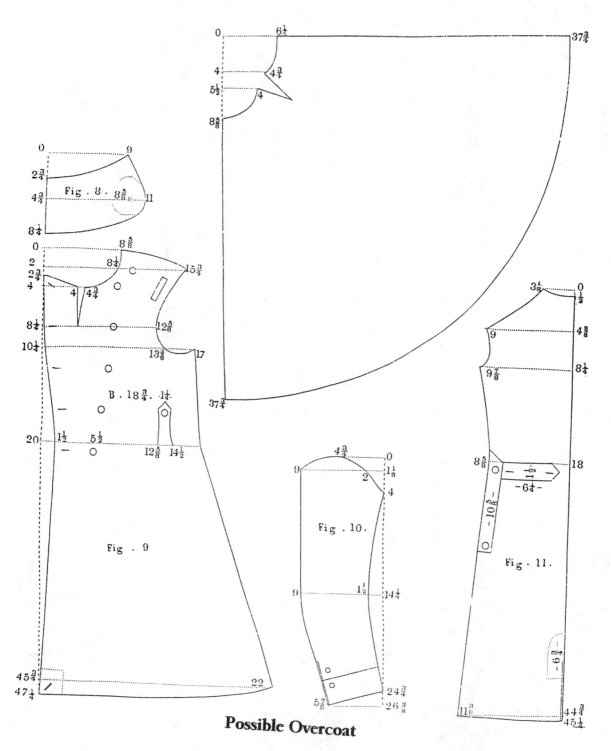

Possible Overcoat

Shoulder Straps for Officers

Length of Strap, 4 inches—Width, 1½ inches—Width of Embroidery, ⅜ inch.
FOR GENERAL STAFF OFFICERS—on Dark Blue Cloth.
FOR INFANTRY, OFFICERS—on Saxony Blue Cloth.
FOR ARTILLERY OFFICERS—on Scarlet Cloth.
FOR RIFLE OFFICERS—on Green Cloth.
FOR CAVALRY OFFICERS—on Yellow Cloth.
FOR DRAGOON OFFICERS—on Orange Cloth.

COLONEL—Silver Embroidered Eagle.

GENERAL-IN-CHIEF—3 Silver Embroidered Stars.

CAPTAIN—2 Gold Embroidered Bars at each end.

MAJOR-GENERAL—2 Silver Embroidered Stars.

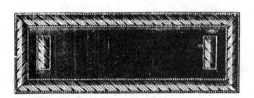

1st LIEUTENANT—1 Gold Emb'd Bar at each end.

BRIGADIER-GENERAL—1 Silver Embroidered Star.

2d LIEUTENANT.

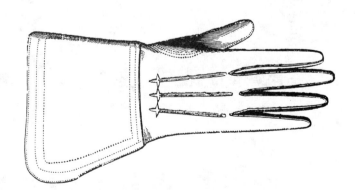

Gauntlets—Buff or White.

210

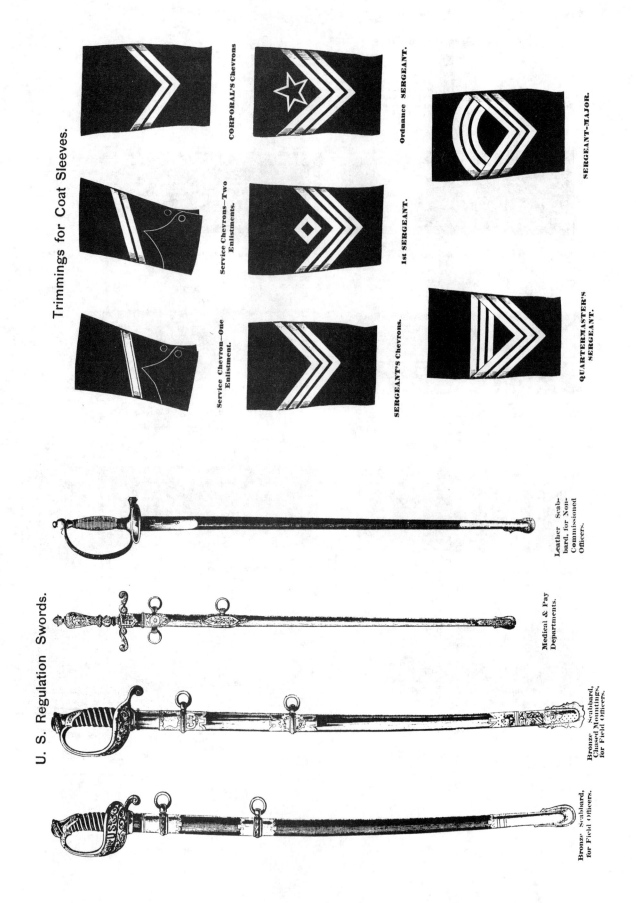

Trimmings for Coat Sleeves.

CORPORAL'S Chevrons.

Ordnance SERGEANT.

SERGEANT-MAJOR.

Service Chevrons—Two Enlistments.

1st SERGEANT.

Service Chevron—One Enlistment.

SERGEANT'S Chevrons.

QUARTERMASTER'S SERGEANT.

U. S. Regulation Swords.

Leather Scabbard, for Non-Commissioned Officers.

Medical & Pay Departments.

Bronze Scabbard, Chased Mountings, for Field Officers.

Bronze Scabbard, for Field Officers.

Chapeaux, Hats, and Caps.

U. S. A. Regulation Chapeau.

U. S. Felt Hat.

Fatigue Cap, with Oiled
Silk Cover.

Fatigue Cap, with Gold,
or Silk Braid.

Burnside Pattern Felt Hat.

Artillery Cap.

Hat and Cap Ornaments for Officers.

STAFF.

INFANTRY.

ARTILLERY.

CAVALRY.

Cavalry company grade officer (below) wearing uniform single-breasted frock coat with epaulets, Hardee hat and sash.

Infantry, field grade officer (above) wearing uniform double-breasted frock coat with epaulets, Hardee hat and sash.

Infantry private, 4th Battalion Massachusetts Volunteer Militia (below) wearing a chasseur uniform: skirted coat, loose trousers with leggings (tall gaiters) and chasseur-style forage cap.

Infantry private, 5th New York Volunteer (Duryee Zouaves) (above) wearing American Zouave uniform of open jacket, vest, Zouave pantaloons, gaiters, sash, turban and fez.

Foot troops (infantry, heavy artillery, etc,) private (below) wearing greatcoat and chasseur-style forage cap.

Infantry sergeant (above) wearing uniform single-breasted frock coat with NCO shoulder scales and holding a Hardee hat.

Cavalry private (below) in uniform 'shell' jacket with shoulder scales, double-seated mounted trousers and Hardee hat.

Infantry private (above) wearing sack coat and forage cap (kepi) with the basic infantryman's accouterments.

216

UNIFORM OF BLENKER'S 8TH
NEW YORK VOLUNTEERS.

UNIFORM OF THE GARI-
BALDI GUARDS.
COLONEL D'UTASSY.

UNIFORM OF THE NATIONAL
RIFLES. FROM A PHOTOGRAPH.

UNIFORM OF THE SIXTH
MASSACHUSETTS.
FROM A PHOTOGRAPH.

FATIGUE UNIFORM AND KILTS
OF THE 79TH NEW YORK.

UNIFORM OF THE 1ST MASS.
AT BULL RUN. FROM
A PHOTOGRAPH.

Excerpts from the
Uniform Regulations for the Army of the United States 1861

COAT.

For Commissioned Officers.

1442. All officers shall wear a frock-coat of dark blue cloth, the skirt to extend from two-thirds to three-fourths of the distance from the top of the hip to the bend of the knee; single-breasted for Captains and Lieutenants; double-breasted for all other grades.

1443. *For a Major-General*—two rows of buttons on the breast, nine in each row, placed by threes; the distance between each row, five and one-half inches at top, and three and one-half inches at bottom; stand-up collar, to rise no higher than to permit the chin to turn freely over it, to hook in front at the bottom, and slope thence up and backward at an angle of thirty degrees on each side; cuffs two and one-half inches deep to go around the sleeves parallel with the lower edge, and to button with three small buttons at the under seam; pockets in the folds of the skirts, with one button at the hip, and one at the end of each pocket, making four buttons on the back and skirt of the coat, the hip button to range with the lowest buttons on the breast; collar and cuffs to be of dark blue velvet; lining of the coat black.

1444. *For a Brigadier-General*—the same as for a Major-General, except that there will be only eight buttons in each row on the breast, placed in pairs.

1445. *For a Colonel*—the same as for a Major-General, except that there will be only seven buttons in each row on the breast, placed at equal distances; collar and cuffs of the same color and material as the coat.

1446. *For a Lieutenant-Colonel*—the same as for a Colonel.

1447. *For a Major*—the same as for a Colonel.

1448. *For a Captain*—the same as for a Colonel, except that there will be only one row of nine buttons on the breast, placed at equal distances.

1449. *For a First Lieutenant*—the same as for a Captain.

1450. *For a Second Lieutenant*—the same as for a Captain.

1451. *For a Brevet Second Lieutenant*—the same as for a Captain.

1452. *For a Medical Cadet*—the same as for a Brevet Second Lieutenant.

1453. A round jacket, according to pattern, of dark blue cloth, trimmed with scarlet, with the Russian shoulder-knot, the prescribed insignia of rank to be worked in silver in the centre of the knot, may be worn on undress duty by officers of Light Artillery.

For Enlisted Men.

1454. The uniform coat for all enlisted *foot* men, shall be a single-breasted frock of dark blue cloth, made without plaits, with a skirt extending one-half the distance from the top of the hip to the bend of the knee; one row of nine buttons on the breast, placed at equal distances; stand-up collar to rise no higher than to permit the chin to turn freely over it, to hook in front at the bottom and then to slope up and backward at an angle of thirty degrees on each side; cuffs pointed according to pattern, and to button with two small buttons at the under seam; collar and cuffs edged with a cord or welt of cloth as follows, to wit: Scarlet *for Artillery;* sky-blue *for Infantry;* yellow *for Engineers;* crimson *for Ordnance* and *Hospital stewards.* On each shoulder a metallic scale according to pattern; narrow lining for skirt of the coat of the same color and material as the coat; pockets in the folds of the skirts with one button at each hip to range with the lowest buttons on the breast; no buttons at the ends of the pockets.

1455. *All Enlisted Men of the Cavalry and Light Artillery* shall wear a uniform jacket of dark blue cloth, with one row of twelve small buttons on the breast placed at equal distances; stand-up collar to rise no higher than to permit the chin to turn freely over it, to hook in front at the bottom, and to slope the same as the coat-collar; on the collar, on each side, two blind button-holes of lace, three-eighths of an inch wide, one small button on the button-hole, lower button-hole extending back four inches, upper button-hole three and a half inches; top button and front ends of collar bound with lace three-eighths of an inch wide, and a strip of the same extending down the front and around the whole lower edge of the jacket; the back seam laced with the same, and on the cuff a point of the same shape as that on the coat, but formed of the lace; jacket to extend to the waist, and to be lined with white flannel; two small buttons at the under seam of the cuff, as on the coat cuff; one hook and eye at the bottom of the collar; color of lace (worsted), yellow for *Cavalry,* and scarlet for *Light Artillery.*

1456. *For all Musicians*—the same as for other enlisted men of their respective corps, with the addition of a facing of lace three-eighths of an inch wide on the front of the *coat or jacket,* made in the following manner: bars of three-eighths of an inch worsted lace placed on a line with each button six and one-half inches wide at the bottom, and *thence* gradually expanding upward to the last button, counting from the waist up, and contracting from thence to the bottom of the collar, where it will be six and one-half inches wide, with a strip of the same lace following the bars at their outer extremity—the whole presenting something of what is called the herring-bone form; the color of the lace facing to correspond with the color of the trimming of the corps.

1457. *For Fatigue Purposes*—a sack coat of dark blue flannel extending half-way down the thigh, and made loose, without sleeve or body lining, falling collar, inside pocket on the left side, four coat buttons down the front.

1458. *For Recruits*—the sack coat will be made with sleeve and body lining, the latter of flannel.

1459. On all occasions of duty, except fatigue, and when out of quarters, the coat or jacket shall be buttoned and hooked at the collar.

BUTTONS.

1460. *For General Officers and Officers of the General Staff*—gilt, convex, with spread eagle and stars, and plain border; large size, seven-eighths of an inch in exterior diameter; small size, one-half inch.

1461. *For Officers of the Corps of Engineers*—gilt, nine-tenths of an inch in exterior diameter, slightly convex; a raised bright rim, one-thirtieth of an inch wide; device, an eagle holding in his beak a scroll, with the word "*Essayons*," a bastion with embrasures in the distance surrounded by water, with a rising sun—the figures to be of dead gold upon a bright field. Small buttons of the same form and device, and fifty-five hundredths of an inch in exterior diameter.

1462. *For Officers of the Corps of Topographical Engineers*—gilt, seven-eighths of an inch exterior diameter, convex and solid; device, the shield of the United States, occupying one-half the diameter, and the letters 𝕿. 𝕰. in old English characters the other half; small buttons, one-half inch diameter, device and form the same.

1463. *For Officers of the Ordnance Department*—gilt, convex, plain border, cross cannon and bombshell, with a circular scroll over and across the cannon, containing the words "Ordnance Corps;" large size, seven-eighths of an inch in exterior diameter; small size, one-half inch.

1464. *For Officers of Artillery, Infantry, and Cavalry*—gilt, convex; device, a spread eagle with the letter A, for Artillery—I, for Infantry—C, for Cavalry, on the shield; large size, seven-eighths of an inch in exterior diameter; small size, one-half inch.

1465. *Aides-de-camp* may wear the button of the General Staff, or of their regiment or corps, at their option.

1466. *For Medical Cadets*—same as for Officers of the General Staff.

1467. *For all Enlisted Men*—yellow, the same as is used by the Artillery, &c., omitting the letter in the shield.

TROWSERS.

1468. *For General Officers and Officers of the Ordnance Department* —of dark blue cloth, plain, without stripe, welt, or cord down the outer seam.

1469. *For Officers of the General Staff and Staff Corps*, except the Ordnance—dark blue cloth, with a gold cord, one-eighth of an inch in diameter, along the outer seam.

1470. *For all Regimental Officers*—dark blue cloth, with a welt let into the outer seam, one-eighth of an inch in diameter, of colors corresponding to the facings of the respective regiments, viz.: *Cavalry*, yellow; *Artillery*, scarlet; *Infantry*, sky-blue.

1471. *For Medical Cadets*—same as for Officers of the General Staff, except a welt of buff cloth, instead of a gold cord.

1472. *For Enlisted Men*, except companies of Light Artillery—dark blue cloth; *sergeants* with a stripe one and one-half inch wide; *corporals* with a stripe one-half inch wide, of worsted lace, down and over the outer seam, of the color of the facings of the respective corps.

1473. *Ordnance Sergeants and Hospital Stewards*—stripe of crimson lace one and one-half inch wide.

1474. *Privates*—plain, without stripe or welt.

1475. *For Companies of Artillery equipped as Light Artillery*—sky-blue cloth.

All trowsers to be made loose, without plaits, and to spread well over the boot; to be re-enforced for all enlisted mounted men.

HAT.

1476. *For Officers*—of best black felt. The dimensions of medium size to be as follows:

> Width of brim, 3¼ inches.
> Height of crown, 6¼ inches.
> Oval of tip, ½ inch.
> Taper of crown, ¾ inch.
> Curve of head, ⅜ inch.

The binding to be ½ inch deep, of best black ribbed silk.

1477. *For Enlisted Men*—of black felt, same shape and size as for officers, with double row of stitching, instead of binding, around the edge. To agree in quality with the pattern deposited in the clothing arsenal.

1478. *Medical Cadets* will wear a forage cap according to pattern.

221

Trimmings.

1479. *For General Officers*—gold cord, with acorn-shaped ends. The brim of the hat looped up on the right side, and fastened with an eagle attached to the side of the hat; three black ostrich-feathers on the left side; a gold-embroidered wreath in front, on black velvet ground, encircling the letters 𝕌. 𝕊. in silver, old English characters.

1480. *For Officers of the Adjutant-General's, Inspector-General's, Quartermaster's, Subsistence, Medical and Pay Departments, and the Judge Advocate, above the rank of Captain*—the same as for General Officers, except the cord, which will be of black silk and gold.

1481. *For the same Departments, below the rank of Field Officers*—the same as for Field Officers, except that there will be but two feathers.

1482. *For Officers of the Corps of Engineers*—the same as for the General Staff, except the ornament in front, which will be a gold-embroidered wreath of laurel and palm, encircling a silver turreted castle on black velvet ground.

1483. *For Officers of the Topographical Engineers*—the same as for the General Staff, except the ornament in front, which will be a gold-embroidered wreath of oak leaves, encircling a gold-embroidered shield, on black velvet ground.

1484. *For Officers of the Ordnance Department*—the same as for the General Staff, except the ornament in front, which will be a gold-embroidered shell and flame, on black velvet ground.

1485. *For Officers of Cavalry*—the same as for the General Staff, except the ornament in front, which will be two gold-embroidered sabres crossed, edges upward, on black velvet ground, with the number of the regiment in silver in the upper angle.

1486. *For Officers of Artillery*—the same as for the General Staff, except the ornament in front, which will be gold-embroidered cross-cannon, on black velvet ground, with the number of the regiment in silver at the intersection of the cross-cannon.

1487. *For Officers of Infantry*—the same as for Artillery, except the ornament in front, which will be a gold-embroidered bugle, on black velvet ground, with the number of the regiment in silver within the bend.

1488. *For Enlisted Men, except companies of Light Artillery*—the same as for officers of the respective corps, except that there will be but one feather, the cord will be of worsted, of the same color as that of the facing of the corps, three-sixteenths of an inch in diameter, running three times through a slide of the same material, and terminating with two tassels, not less than two inches long, on the side of the hat opposite the feather. The insignia of corps, in brass, in front of the hat, corresponding with those prescribed for officers, with the number of regiment, five-eighths of an inch long, in brass, and letter of company, one inch, in brass, arranged over insignia.

1489. *For Hospital Stewards* the cord will be of buff and green mixed. The wreath in front of brass, with the letters U. S. in Roman, of white metal. Brim to be looped up to side of hat with a brass eagle, having a hook attached to the bottom to secure the brim—on the right side for mounted men and left side for foot men. The feather to be worn on the side opposite the loop.

1490. All the trimmings of the hat are to be made so that they can be detached; but the eagle, badge of corps, and letter of company, are to be always worn.

1491. For companies of Artillery equipped as Light Artillery, the old pattern uniform cap, with red horsehair plume, cord and tassel.

1492. Officers of the General Staff, and Staff Corps, may wear, at their option, a light French chapeau, either stiff crown or flat, according to the pattern deposited in the Adjutant-General's office. Officers below the rank of field officers to wear but two feathers.

FORAGE CAPS.

1493. For fatigue purposes, forage caps, of pattern in the Quartermaster-General's office: dark blue cloth, with a welt of the same around the crown, and yellow metal letters in front to designate companies.

1494. Commissioned officers may wear forage caps of the same pattern, with the distinctive ornament of the corps and regiment in front.

CRAVAT OR STOCK.

1495. *For all Officers*—black; when a cravat is worn, the tie not to be visible at the opening of the collar.

1496. *For all Enlisted Men*—black leather, according to pattern.

BOOTS.

1497. *For all Officers*—ankle or Jefferson.

1498. *For Enlisted Men of Cavalry and Light Artillery*—ankle and Jefferson, rights and lefts, according to pattern.

1499. *For Enlisted Men of Artillery, Infantry, Engineers, and Ordnance*—Jefferson, rights and lefts, according to pattern.

SPURS.

1500. *For all Mounted Officers*—yellow metal, or gilt.

1501. *For all Enlisted Mounted Men*—yellow metal, according to pattern.

GLOVES.

1502. *For General Officers and Officers of the General Staff and Staff Corps*—buff or white.

1503. *For Officers of Artillery, Infantry, Cavalry, Dragoons, and Riflemen*—white.

SASH.

1504. *For General Officers*—buff, silk net, with silk bullion fringe ends; sash to go twice around the waist, and to tie behind the left hip, pendent part not to extend more than eighteen inches below the tie.

1505. *For Officers of the Adjutant-General's, Inspector-General's, Quartermaster's, and Subsistence Departments, Corps of Engineers, Topographical Engineers, Ordnance, Artillery, Infantry, Cavalry, and the Judge Advocate of the Army*—crimson silk net; *for Officers of the Medical Department*—medium or emerald green silk net, with silk bullion fringe ends; to go around the waist and tie as for General Officers.

1506. *For all Sergeant Majors, Quartermaster Sergeants, Ordnance Sergeants, Hospital Stewards, First Sergeants, Principal or Chief Musicians and Chief Buglers*—red worsted sash, with worsted bullion fringe ends; to go twice around the waist, and to tie behind the left hip, pendent part not to extend more than eighteen inches below the tie.

1507. The sash will be worn (over the coat) on all occasions of duty of every description, except stable and fatigue.

1508. The sash will be worn by " *Officers of the Day*" across the body, scarf fashion, from the right shoulder to the left side, instead of around the waist, tying behind the left hip as prescribed.

SWORD-BELT.

1509. *For all Officers*—a waist-belt not less than one and one-half inch nor more than two inches wide to be worn over the sash; the sword to be suspended from it by slings of the same material as the belt, with a hook attached to the belt upon which the sword may be hung.

1510. *For General Officers* — Russia leather, with three stripes of gold embroidery; the slings embroidered on both sides.

1511. *For all other Officers*—black leather, plain.

1512. *For all Non-commissioned Officers*—black leather, plain.

SWORD-BELT PLATE.

1513. *For all Officers and Enlisted Men*—gilt, rectangular, two inches wide, with a raised bright rim; a silver wreath of laurel encircling the "Arms of the United States;" eagle, shield, scroll, edge of cloud and rays bright. The motto, "E PLURIBUS UNUM," in silver letters, upon the scroll; stars also of silver; according to pattern.

SWORD AND SCABBARD.

1514. *For General Officers*—straight sword, gilt hilt, silver grip, brass or steel scabbard.

1515. *For Officers of the Adjutant-General's, Inspector-General's, Quartermaster's, and Subsistence Departments, Corps of Engineers, Topographical Engineers, Ordnance, the Judge Advocate of the Army, Aides-de-Camp, Field Officers of Artillery, Infantry, and Foot Riflemen, and for the Light Artillery*—the sword of the pattern adopted by the War Department, April 9, 1850; or the one described in General Orders No. 21, of August 28, 1860, for officers therein designated.

1516. *For the Medical and Pay Departments*—small sword and scabbard, according to pattern in the Surgeon-General's office.

1517. *For Medical Cadets*, the sword and belt and plate will be the same as for non-commissioned officers.

1518. *For Officers of Cavalry*—sabre and scabbard now in use, according to pattern in the Ordnance Department.

1519. *For the Artillery, Infantry, and Foot Riflemen*, except the field officers—the sword of the pattern adopted by the War Department, April 9, 1850.

1520. The sword and sword-belt will be worn upon all occasions of duty, without exception.

1521. When on foot, the sabre will be suspended from the hook attached to the belt.

1522. When not on military duty, officers may wear swords of honor, or the prescribed sword, with a scabbard, gilt, or of leather with gilt mountings.

SWORD-KNOT.

1523. *For General Officers*—gold cord with acorn end.
1524. *For all other officers*—gold lace strap with gold bullion tassel.

BADGES TO DISTINGUISH RANK.

Epaulettes.

1525. *For the Major-General Commanding the Army*—gold, with solid crescent; device, three silver-embroidered stars, one, one and a half inches in diameter, one, one and one-fourth inches in diameter, and one, one and one-eighth inches in diameter, placed on the strap in a row, longitudinally, and equidistant, the largest star in the centre of the crescent, the smallest at the top; dead and bright gold bullion, one-half inch in diameter and three and one-half inches long.

1526. *For all other Major-Generals*—the same as for the Major-General Commanding the Army, except that there will be two stars on the strap instead of three, omitting the smallest.

1527. *For a Brigadier-General*—the same as for a Major-General, except that, instead of two, there shall be one star (omitting the smallest) placed upon the strap, and not within the crescent.

1528. *For a Colonel*—the same as for a Brigadier-General, substituting a silver-embroidered spread eagle for the star upon the strap; and within the crescent for the *Medical Department*—a laurel wreath embroidered in gold, and the letters 𝕸. 𝕾., in old English characters, in silver, within the wreath; *Pay Department*—same as the Medical Department, with the letters 𝕻. 𝕯., in old English characters; *Corps of Engineers*—a turreted castle of silver; *Corps of Topographical Engineers*—a shield embroidered in gold, and below it the letters 𝕿. 𝕰., in old English characters, in silver; *Ordnance Department*—shell and flame in silver embroidery; *Regimental Officers*—the number of the regiment embroidered in gold, within a circlet of embroidered silver, one and three-fourths inches in diameter, upon cloth of the following colors: *for Artillery*—scarlet; *Infantry*—light or sky blue; *Cavalry*—yellow.

1529. *For a Lieutenant-Colonel*—the same as for a Colonel, according to corps, but substituting for the eagle a silver-embroidered leaf.

1530. *For a Major*—the same as for a Colonel, according to corps, omitting the eagle.

1531 *For a Captain*—the same as for a Colonel, according to corps, except that the bullion will be only one-fourth of an inch in diameter, and two and one half inches long, and substituting for the eagle two silver-embroidered bars.

1532. *For a First Lieutenant*—the same as for a Colonel, according to corps, except that the bullion will be only one-eighth of an inch in diameter, and two and one-half inches long, and substituting for the eagle one silver-embroidered bar.

1533. *For a Second Lieutenant*—the same as for a First Lieutenant, omitting the bar.

1534. *For a Brevet Second Lieutenant*—the same as for a Second Lieutenant.

1535. All officers having military rank will wear an epaulette on each shoulder.

1536. The epaulette may be dispensed with when not on duty, and on certain duties off parade, to wit: at drills, at inspections of barracks and hospitals, on Courts of Inquiry and Boards, at inspections of articles and necessaries, on working parties and fatigue duties, and upon the march, except when, in war, there is immediate expectation of meeting the enemy, and also when the overcoat is worn.

Shoulder-Straps.

1537. *For the Major-General Commanding the Army*—dark blue cloth, one and three-eighths inches wide by four inches long; bordered with an embroidery of gold one-fourth of an inch wide; three silver-embroidered stars of five rays, one star on the centre of the strap, and one on each side equidistant between the centre and the outer edge of the strap; the centre star to be the largest.

1538. *For all other Major-Generals*—the same as for the Major-General Commanding the Army, except that there will be two stars instead of three; the centre of each star to be one inch from the outer edge of the gold embroidery on the ends of the strap; both stars of the same size.

1539. *For a Brigadier-General*—the same as for a Major-General, except that there will be one star instead of two; the centre of the star to be equidistant from the outer edge of the embroidery on the ends of the strap.

1540. *For a Colonel*—the same size as for a Major-General, and bordered in like manner with an embroidery of gold; a silver-embroidered spread eagle on the centre of the strap, two inches between the tips of the wings, having in the right talon an olive-branch, and in the left a bundle of arrows; an escutcheon on the breast, as represented in the arms of the United States; cloth of the strap as follows: for the *General Staff and Staff Corps*—dark blue; *Artillery*—scarlet; *Infantry*—light or sky blue; *Cavalry*—yellow.

1541. *For a Lieutenant-Colonel*—the same as for a Colonel, according to corps, omitting the eagle, and introducing a silver-embroidered leaf at each end, each leaf extending seven-eighths of an inch from the end border of the strap.

1542. *For a Major*—the same as for a Colonel, according to corps, omitting the eagle, and introducing a gold-embroidered leaf at each end, each leaf extending seven-eighths of an inch from the end border of the strap.

1543. *For a Captain*—the same as for a Colonel, according to corps, omitting the eagle, and introducing at each end two gold-embroidered bars of the same width as the border, placed parallel to the ends of the strap; the distance between them and from the border equal to the width of the border.

1544. *For a First Lieutenant*—the same as for a Colonel, according to corps, omitting the eagle, and introducing at each end one gold-embroidered bar of the same width as the border, placed parallel to the ends of the strap, at a distance from the border equal to its width.

1545. *For a Second Lieutenant*—the same as for a Colonel, according to corps, omitting the eagle.

1546. *For a Brevet Second Lieutenant*—the same as for a Second Lieutenant.

1547. *For a Medical Cadet*—a strip of gold lace three inches long, half an inch wide, placed in the middle of a strap of green cloth three and three-quarter inches long by one and one-quarter inches wide.

1548. The shoulder-strap will be worn whenever the epaulette is not.

Chevrons.

1549. The rank of non-commissioned officers will be marked by chevrons upon both sleeves of the uniform coat and overcoat, above the elbow, of silk or worsted binding one-half an inch wide, same color as the edging on the coat, points down, as follows:

1550. *For a Sergeant Major*—three bars and an arc, in silk.

1551. *For a Quartermaster Sergeant*—three bars and a tie, in silk.

1552. *For an Ordnance Sergeant*—three bars and a star, in silk.

1553. *For a Hospital Steward*—a half chevron of the following description,—viz.: of emerald green cloth, one and three-fourths inches wide, running obliquely downward from the outer to the inner seam of the sleeve, and at an angle of about thirty degrees with a horizontal, parallel to, and one-eighth of an inch distant from, both the upper and lower edge, an embroidery of yellow silk one-eighth of an inch wide, and in the centre a "caduceus" two inches long, embroidered also with yellow silk, the head toward the outer seam of the sleeve.

1554. *For a First Sergeant*— three bars and a lozenge, in worsted

1555. *For a Sergeant*—three bars, in worsted.

1556. *For a Corporal*—two bars, in worsted.

1557. *For a Pioneer*—two crossed hatchets of cloth, same color and material as the edging of the collar, to be sewed on each arm above the elbow in the place indicated for a chevron (those of a corporal to be just above and resting on the chevron), the head of the hatchet upward, its edge outward, of the following dimensions, viz.: *Handle*—four and one-half inches long, one-fourth to one-third of an inch wide. *Hatchet*—two inches long, one inch wide at the edge.

1558. *To indicate service*—all non-commissioned officers, musicians, and privates, who have served faithfully for the term of five years, will wear, as a mark of distinction, upon both sleeves of the uniform coat, below the elbow, a diagonal half chevron, one-half an inch wide, extending from seam to seam, the front end nearest the cuff, and one-half an inch above the point of the cuff, to be of the same color as the edging on the coat. In like manner, an additional half chevron, above and parallel to the first, for every subsequent five years of faithful service; distance between each chevron one-fourth of an inch. Service in war will be indicated by a light or sky blue stripe on each side of the chevron for Artillery, and a red stripe for all other corps the stripe to be one-eighth of an inch wide.

OVERCOAT.
For Commissioned Officers.

1559. A "*cloak coat*" of dark blue cloth, closing by means of four frog buttons of black silk and loops of black silk cord down the breast, and at the throat by a long loop *à échelle*, without tassel or plate, on the left side, and a black silk frog button on the right; cord for the loops fifteen-hundredths of an inch in diameter; back, a single piece, slit up from the bottom, from fifteen to seventeen inches, according to the height of the wearer, and closing at will, by buttons, and button-holes cut in a concealed flap; collar of the same color and material as the coat, rounded at the edges, and to stand or fall; when standing, to be about five inches high; sleeves loose, of a single piece, and round at the bottom, without cuff or slit; lining, woolen; around the front and lower border, the edges of the pockets, the edges of the sleeves, collar, and slit in the back, a flat braid of black silk one-half an inch wide; and around each frog button on the breast, a knot two and one-quarter inches in diameter of black silk cord, seven-hundredths of an inch in diameter, arranged according to drawing; cape of the same color and material as the coat, removable at the pleasure of the wearer, and reaching to the cuff of the coat-sleeve when the arm is extended; coat to extend down the leg from six to eight inches below the knee, according to height. *To indicate rank*, there will be on both sleeves, near the lower edge, a knot of flat black silk braid not exceeding one-eighth of an inch in width, arranged according to drawing, and composed as follows:

1560. *For a General*—of five braids, double knot.

1561. *For a Colonel*—of five braids, single knot.

1562. *For a Lieutenant-Colonel*—of four braids, single knot.

1563. *For a Major*—of three braids, single knot.

1564. *For a Captain*—of two braids, single knot.

1565. *For a First Lieutenant*—of one braid, single knot.

1566. *For a Second Lieutenant and Brevet Second Lieutenant*—a plain sleeve, without knot or ornament.

For Enlisted Men.

1567. *Of all Mounted Corps*—of sky-blue cloth; stand-and-fall collar; double-breasted; cape to reach down to the cuff of the coat when the arm is extended, and to button all the way up; buttons (1467).

1568. *All other Enlisted Men*—of sky-blue cloth; stand-up collar; single-breasted; cape to reach down to the elbows when the arm is extended, and to button all the way up; buttons (1467).

1569. *For Cavalry*—a gutta-percha talma, or cloak extending to the knee, with long sleeves.

OTHER ARTICLES OF CLOTHING AND EQUIPMENT.

1570. *Flannel shirt, drawers, stockings, and stable-frock*—the same as now furnished.

1571. *Blanket*—woolen, gray, with letters U. S. in black, four inches long, in the centre; to be seven feet long, and five and a half feet wide, and to weigh five pounds.

1572. *Canvas overalls for Engineer soldiers*—of white cotton; one garment to cover the whole of the body below the waist, the breast, the shoulders, and the arms; sleeves loose, to allow a free play of the arms, with narrow wristband buttoning with one button; overalls to fasten at the neck behind with two buttons, and at the waist behind with buckle and tongue.

1573. *Belts of all Enlisted Men*—black leather.

1574. *Cartridge-box*—according to pattern in the Ordnance Department.

1575. *Drum-sling*—white webbing; to be provided with a brass drum-stick carriage, according to pattern.

1576. *Knapsack*—of painted canvas, according to pattern now issued by the Quartermaster's Department; the great-coat, when carried, to be neatly folded, not rolled, and covered by the outer flap of the knapsack.

1577. *Haversack*—of painted canvas, with an inside sack unpainted, according to the pattern now issued by the Quartermaster's Department.

1578. *Canteen*—of tin, covered with woolen cloth, of the pattern now issued by the Quartermaster's Department.

1628. General Officers, and Colonels having the brevet rank of General Officers, may, on occasions of ceremony, and when not serving with troops, wear the "dress" and "undress" prescribed by existing regulations.

1629. Officers below the grade of Colonel having brevet rank, will wear the epaulettes and shoulder-straps distinctive of their army rank. In all other respects, their uniform and dress will be that of their respective regiments, corps, or departments, and according to their commissions in the same. Officers above the grade of Lieutenant-Colonel by ordinary commission, having brevet rank, may wear the uniform of their respective regiments or corps, or that of General Officers, according to their brevet rank.

1630. The uniform and dress of the Signal Officer will be that of a Major of the General Staff.

1631. Officers are permitted to wear a plain dark blue body-coat, with the button designating their respective corps, regiments, or departments, without any other mark or ornament upon it. Such a coat, however, is not to be considered as a dress for any military purpose.

1632. In like manner, officers are permitted to wear a buff, white, or blue vest, with the small button of their corps, regiment, or department.

1633. Officers serving with mounted troops are allowed to wear, for stable duty, a plain dark blue cloth jacket, with one or two rows of buttons down the front, according to rank; stand-up collar, sloped in front as that of the uniform coat; shoulder-straps according to rank, but no other ornament.

1634. The hair to be short; the beard to be worn at the pleasure of the individual; but, when worn, to be kept short and neatly trimmed.

1635. *A Band* will wear the uniform of the regiment or corps to which it belongs. The commanding officer may, at the expense of the corps, sanctioned by the Council of Administration, make such *additions* in ornaments as he may judge proper.

Seventh Regiment

National Guard, State of New York

Notes on the 7th Regiment
by Peter Dervis

The uniform of the Seventh Regiment New York National Guard may not have been the showiest dress ever worn by America's citizen soldiers, however it certainly was one of the most distinctive and probably the most copied. The somber gray coatee was introduced in 1824 and became the symbol of the nation's crack citizen force. One regimental historian has even linked it to the adoption of gray uniforms by the Confederacy. By the middle 1870s units as far afield as Chicago, Connecticut, Roxbury,MA, and Burlington, VT, as well as several other New York City regiments, were wearing a uniform based on that of the Seventh Regiment.

Aside from its color, the essential elements of the 'Seventh' uniform, including the shako, coatee, epaulets, beltplate, cartridge box, crossbelts, waistbelt, buckle, and white or colored trousers were common to the vast majority of militia units until Federal style uniforms made their appearance during the 1870s and 1880s. A number of units continued to turn out their personnel in this style of dress until the outbreak of the Second World War. The 107th Infantry, the Seventh Regiment's lineal descendant, had a 'color party' wearing this uniform into the 1980s.

Thus it seems fitting that this style of uniform, which was so prevalent at the outbreak of the Civil War, should be described in a book dealing with the fashion of that period. It should be noted at the outset that this style of uniform was very different from that described in the *Uniform Regulations for the Army of the United States 1861*. The body coat, or coatee, had disappeared from the US army dress, except for the cadets at West Point, in 1851 when the army adopted a frock coat for all troops. A short 'uniform jacket' was introduced for mounted men in 1854. However, most militia units, classified as infantry, clung to the older style garment often surmounted by an equally old fashioned headdress, such as a tall shako or bearskin cap.

Of course this was not the uniform worn by units in the field during the Civil War. However, even on active service, the militia man frequently differed from the regular uniform. Here again the Seventh Regiment was distinctive and a trend setter. Fatigue dress consisted of a gray kepi with black trim, gray shell jacket with black trim and gray trousers with a black stripe. Interestingly a number of units which wore the gray full dress also adopted this rather than the blue fatigue blouse, not withstanding the South's widespread adoption of gray as a uniform color. Ironically, this was the uniform worn by the Seventh during their tour of active duty in Washington, DC at the outbreak of the war in 1861.

After the Civil War many units, including the Seventh Regiment, abandoned the coatee in favor of a more modern and workmanlike jacket. But, after two years the Seventh Regiment resumed the coatee which remained their full dress uniform thereafter. Actually the coatee made something of a comeback after the war and resumed its place as the garment of choice for many fashionable militia organizations. Perhaps the militia and National Guard units preferred to wear something which distinguished them from the regulars in their sober blue uniforms.

The following is the 'Bill of Dress' from the *Manual of the Seventh Regiment* published in 1868. The uniforms described, except for the size and shape of the shako, represent a return to the style of full dress that had been worn by the regiment until 1861.

As there were no patterns or schematic drawings of the uniforms, Civil War era photographs have been used to illustrate the regiment's dress. Included, as well, is a drawing of the short lived chasseur uniform worn from 1865-1868. The uniforms depicted are those worn just before and during the outbreak of hostilities. Minor variations occurred in the fatigue dress during the war, such as the substitution of black belts for the white belts previously worn. Although these uniforms are specific unto the Seventh Regiment, they are typical of the type of uniform worn by many units both before and after the Civil War.

Chasseur uniform, illustrated by H. A. Ogden, is similar to the pattern worn by other units during the Civil War. It was of gray cloth and was adopted by the 7th Regiment after the Civil War. However, it proved to be unpopular with the regiment and was replaced in 1868 by the coatee and trousers, the old shako being replaced by a small low crowned model with a pom-pom.

Enlisted man circa 1860-61 (below) wearing full dress coatee & shako. The tall cylindrical shako was replaced by a smaller low crowned model after the war. White trousers were worn in summer. The boy wears a Zouave outfit.

Company grade officer, Captain George T. Haws (above) wears a single breasted blue frock coat and kepi, with regimental gray trousers. Officers in full dress wore gray uniforms, but their undress uniform was blue with gray trousers. The shoulder straps with a red field commemorated the regiments artillery origins.

Enlisted man circa 1861 (below) wearing gray fatigue jacket, trousers & kepi. The number '8' represents the company to which he belonged.

Enlisted man circa 1861 (above) in full marching order with greatcoat and pack. The bursting bomb badge on his kepi and his black belt show that he is in Company K , originally the Engineer Company. Later the entire regiment adopted the 'bomb' as the central motif of its badge.

March of the 7th New York - April 1861

BILL OF DRESS

FOR

NON-COMMISSIONED OFFICERS AND PRIVATES,

AS REVISED IN 1867.

UNIFORM COAT.

CADET mixed cloth, the same in color as used at West Point; single-breasted, standing collar: the collar to meet and be hooked under the chin, with two hooks and eyes, and not cut so high as to prevent the free turning of the chin above it; on each side of the collar, a loop of gold lace, four and one-half inches long, with a small N. G. button on the back end of each loop; the collar to be framed with a single stripe of black mohair binding, five-sixteenths of an inch in width (herring-bone pattern); three rows of large N. G. buttons on the front, ten buttons in each row, the top button of the outer row to be four and one-half inches from the center row (measuring from the eye of each button), and increase in distance to the fourth button from the top, which is to be the greatest distance across, and then diminish gradually with an inward curve to three inches at the bottom; double stripe of black mohair binding, five-sixteenths of an inch wide (herring-bone pattern), laid on one-eighth of an inch apart, to extend from the buttons of the center to those of the outer rows; the sleeves to be cut without cuffs; slash flaps of black cloth on the sleeves, five and one-half inches long scolloped, two inches wide at the curves, and two and one-half inches at the points; four loops of gold lace, five-eighths of an inch wide, at equal distances apart, with a small N. G. button on the outer end of each loop; the skirts to measure one inch less across the top than the strap, and diminish to two and one-quarter inches at the bottom; each back to be one and three-quarter inches at the waist, and two and one-quarter inches at the bottom; two large N. G. buttons at the hip; the skirts lined with black, and turned up with black cloth on both the back and front skirts; the turn-ups on the front to commence at the skirt strap, and on the back two inches below the hip button, the back seam to be closed that distance down, the turn-ups to be one-quarter of an inch at the top, and widen downward to one inch in width at two and one-half inches from the bottom of skirt, then curve out to a point, and meet at two inches up from the bottom of skirts; the turn-ups to form a half circle below and above the points, with gold embroidered flat grenade, on black cloth, two inches long and one and one-quarter inches wide on the points of the turn-ups; a slashed flap of black cloth, seven inches long, scolloped, two inches wide at the curves, and three inches at the points; four loops of gold lace, five-eighths of an inch wide, at equal distance apart, with a small N. G. button on the back end of each loop; the flaps to be placed on the skirts in the center; the upper edges to be two inches below, and ranging with the waist seam; the skirts extending to within five inches of the bend of the knee. All the lace used on any part of the coat to be seven line gold U. S. Army lace.

PROPORTION.—For a man five feet eight or nine inches in height: length of waist, nineteen inches; full length of coat, thirty-four inches; length of breast, from the back collar seam, twenty-seven inches; thirty buttons on the breast.

FATIGUE JACKET.

Of gray cloth (the same as coat), single-breasted, standing collar; nine large N. G. buttons on the front, the collar to meet and be hooked with two hooks and eyes, and to be framed with a single stripe of black mohair binding, five-sixteenths of an inch wide (herring-bone pattern); black cloth shoulder strap, two inches wide, rounded at the top, to be sewed in the sleeve head, and extended to the collar, with a small N. G. button sewed on the shoulder, to button through the strap; sleeves without cuffs; a black cloth strap, six and one-half inches long, and one and five-eighth inches wide, to be placed in the middle of the upper sleeve, commencing at the bottom, with three small N. G. buttons placed in the center and at equal distance apart; a black cloth strap, one-half of an inch wide, and lined with leather, to be placed on each hip to support waist belt, to be buttoned with small N. G. button.

PANTS.

Gray cloth (the same as coat), cut straight, with a stripe of black cloth, one and one-half inches wide; the black edge of which to touch the outside seam.

FOR SUMMER.—White duck, cut straight.

OVERCOAT.

Sky-blue, army kersey, with cape, single-breasted, to button from the waist seam up, and seven large N. G. buttons; to be cut large and extend two inches below the bend of the knee. For a man five feet eight to nine inches in height, length of waist, twenty-one inches, full length of coat, forty-three inches; back to be cut sack fashion, width of each back at the hip, four inches; at the bottom, ten inches; and opening up the back seam two-thirds the length of the skirt; two large N. G. buttons on the hip; the side edges in the plait to be pointed and extend downward two-thirds the length of the skirt, with a large N. G. button on and near the bottom and on center of side edges; frock skirt, with waist seams; the width around the bottom of skirt, thirty-three inches; the skirt to lap over in front at bottom about five inches; the height of collar, three and one-half to four inches, to extend up to the ear, and inclose the chin, lap over in front, and button with two small N. G. buttons; the button-holes to be worked through the collar; the cape to be three fourths of a circle, length behind, four inches less than waist, to button up the front with five small N. G. buttons; a button-hole in the cape behind, and a small N. G. button sewed on the back seam of the coat, and button through the cape; the sleeves large, to have a pointed turn-up cuff, two and one half inches deep, with a small N. G. button on the point, the whole width of the sleeve at the hand to be thirteen inches; two pockets in the plaits behind; the body of the coat to be lined with red flannel; the sleeves to be lined with brown linen. No hair, wadding, or padding to be used in any part of the coat.

CHEVRONS.

The rank of Non-commissioned Officers will be designated by chevrons upon both sleeves of the uniform coat. fatigue jacket, and overcoat, above the elbow, as follows:—

SEVENTH REGIMENT.

UNIFORM COAT.—Of gold seven line U. S. Army lace, cushioned upon black cloth, to show one-eighth of an inch of black cloth between the lace.

FATIGUE JACKET.—Of black silk binding, five-eighths of an inch wide, cushioned upon gray cloth, to show one-eighth of an inch of gray cloth between the binding.

OVERCOAT.—Of white worsted binding, five-eighths of an inch wide, laid plain upon the sleeves of the coat, one-eighth of an inch apart.

FOR FIRST SERGEANT.—Three bars and a lozenge.

FOR SERGEANT.—Three bars.

FOR CORPORAL.—Two bars.

All chevrons to be worn points down.

SERVICE CHEVRONS.

Members of the Regiment having served seven years in the corps, will wear on each sleeve of the uniform coat, a diagonal half chevron of two bars of seven line U. S Army lace, cushioned upon black cloth, to show one-eighth of an inch of black cloth between the lace, extending from seam to seam; the front end to be five and one-half inches, and the back end to be nine inches above bottom of sleeve; and, in like manner, an additional bar for every five years of regular service (not honorary) thereafter.

FOR BREVET RANK.—Non-commissioned officers and privates who have received brevet commissions under the provisions of a concurrent resolution passed by the Legislature of 1867, will wear the insignia designating their brevet rank, on the left sleeve of the uniform coat and overcoat, four inches from the wrist.

The badge will be made of black cloth in the shape of a circle, the diameter of which shall be one and one-half inches, with light gold cord around the outside.

In the center of the circle the rank will be inscribed with the same designation as now furnished by the General Regulations of the State, but the insignia being reduced in size to correspond with the size of the circle.

GLOVES.

White cotton.

EPAULETS.

Black doeskin strap, four and one-half inches from crescent; two and one-half inches wide; heavy corded edge to strap; black crescent with one row of one-quarter inch white cotton cord inside, and one row of cord under; white cotton fringe, one-sixteenth of an inch in diameter, and four inches long; small N. G. button; muslin lining; brass hook, one and one-quarter inches long.

UNIFORM CAP.

Body of black felt or beaver, tip pressed in one-quarter of an inch; height in front, four and one-half inches; height behind, seven and one-half inches; width of lower band, one inch; width of upper band, one-half inch in front, slanting to three-quarters of an inch behind; tip of patent leather, diameter four to five and one-half inches; chin-strap of patent leather, one inch wide; visor made of heavy patent leather, double japanned, black on top and dark green on under side, bound with calf-skin, corners rounded, width, one and three-quarter inches; lining of black roan; a button for chin-strap, three quarters of an inch diameter, device, two cannons crossed; center ornament, a medallion figure 7, raised, three-quarters of an inch long, on raised black surface, one inch diameter, inclosed by raised ring, one-eighth of an inch, of miniature balls, surrounded by eight fluted rays, with spear heads thereon and cannons between; total diameter of ornament, two and three-quarter inches; chased ventilator of crescent shape, three-quarters of an inch wide, one-quarter of an inch high, to be placed immediately under the upper band at back of the cap. All ornaments to be gilt.

POMPON.

Of white worsted, three inches in length, two inches in diameter at top, and one inch at bottom. Brass wire shank, three and one-half inches long, with gilt cup.

FATIGUE CAP.

Gray cloth body, with black cloth band; sunken tip, four and three-quarter inches in diameter; height at back, six inches, including band, and two inches in front; black worsted braid round band, tip and up quarters; plain double japanned solid leather visor, without binding, one and three-eighth inches in depth; elastic chin-strap and N. G. buttons at side; three-quarters of an inch gilt figure 7 in front; silk glaze cover, with button-holes.

EQUIPMENTS.

FOR FULL UNIFORM.

BELTS.—Two cross belts of whitened buff leather, two inches wide, with waist belt one and seven-eighth inches wide; the bayonet belt to be connected in the center with a convex brass plate, three and one-quarter inches long, and two and one-quarter inches wide, with the corners cut off; a raised ornamental german silver figure 7, two inches long, to be placed in center of same; waist plate (with French fastening) of plain brass, two and one-quarter inches wide, corners cut off ; a raised german silver Roman letter, one and one-quarter inches long, for Company designation, placed in center of same.

CARTRIDGE-BOX.—Of patent leather ; size of body, six and one-half inches wide and five inches high, one and one-half inches thick, with inside flap ; the outer flap to be eight and one-half inches long and seven and one-half inches wide, scolloped at the bottom, with two plain leather straps and two buckles at the bottom to receive cross belts, and brass knob to fasten flap ; brass cipher letters N. G., with raised figure 7 on center, two inches long and two and one-half inches wide, to be placed on the flap.

BAYONET SCABBARD.—Of plain black leather, eighteen and one-half inches long ; brass top and bottom mountings ; fastened with a brass hook, passing under the throg.

CAP-BOX.—U. S. pattern, with patent leather flap.

SASH.—First Sergeants will wear a sash of red worsted, with worsted bullion tassels, to go twice around the waist and tie behind the left hip ; the pendant part not to extend more than eighteen inches below the tie.

FOR FATIGUE.

BELT.—Black enameled leather, two inches wide ; brass plate (with French fastening) two and one-quarter inches long and two and one-half inches wide, corners cut off, with Company designation engraved in black figure, one and one-half inches long.

CARTRIDGE-BOX.—Body plain leather, six and one-quarter inches long, one and one-quarter inches wide, and three inches high, curved to fit hip, inside flap patent leather, with ends, patent leather outside flap, six and one-half by seven and three-quarter inches, with corners cut off; enameled leather back strap, two and three-quarter inches wide and two inches deep, to run on belt; tin cartridge-box, with partition; brass cipher letters N. G., with raised figure 7 on center, two inches long and two and one-half inches wide, to be placed on the flap.

BAYONET SCABBARD.—To be eighteen inches long, with brass tip and enameled leather throg.

CAP-BOX.—U. S. pattern, with patent leather flap.

SERGEANTS will wear a straight sword; black leather scabbard; gilt cross hilt and mountings, white bone grip, worn through a throg, attached to the waist belt; the sword will be worn on all occasions of duty.

KNAPSACK.

To be made of black enameled leather, sixteen inches wide, twelve and one-half inches high, and three and three-quarter inches deep; the corners to be bound with the same leather; the inside flaps to be of black glazed twilled muslin; two plain black leather straps to be fastened at inside of top of knapsack, one and one-quarter inches wide, to be buckled at bottom; shoulder straps of the same width, to be fastened at center of inside top of knapsack by four copper rivets; the upper portion of the shoulder straps to be fifteen inches long, with two holes to receive brass stud; the right lower strap to be fourteen inches long, to fasten at bottom with buckle; the breast strap to be seventeen inches long and three-quarters of an inch wide, to fasten on each end by brass stud, and connect in center by buckle; three straps on top of knapsack, three-quarters of an inch wide, to buckle around the overcoat when rolled; a white painted number 7 on the outside, three and one-half inches in length.

HAVERSACK.

Enameled leather, twelve inches long, ten inches deep. two and one-half inches wide, with welting in seams; corners rounded; rounded flat to ditto, bound with black roan, with five eighths of an inch strap and buckle; five inches deep; white muslin bag inside; plain leather shoulder strap, four to four and one-half feet long, one and one-quarter inches wide, with black japanned roller buckle.

MISCELLANEOUS.

The caps are not to be worn on one side, but are to be placed even on the men's heads, and brought well down upon the forehead.

The bayonet scabbard and cartridge-box should be placed so as not to be seen in front, and entirely free from contact with the arms. The cross belts crossed well up on the breast, to show only the two upper buttons on the center row of the coat.

The top of the knapsack is to be in line with the bottom of the collar of the coat. In marching order, the overcoat is to be rolled and secured on the top of the knapsack, with straps placed there for that purpose.

When the men are provided with blankets, they will be folded square and placed under the outer straps of the knapsack.

All Non-commissioned Staff Officers are to be armed and equipped in all respects, same as First Sergeants, with the exception prescribed in the appendix to the Bill of Dress for Commissioned Officers.

Commandants of Companies. in their respective commands, are expected to see this Bill of Dress complied with in every particular, and especially that no ornament or designation of rank is worn, except as herein prescribed.

Panorama of
Civil War Era Images

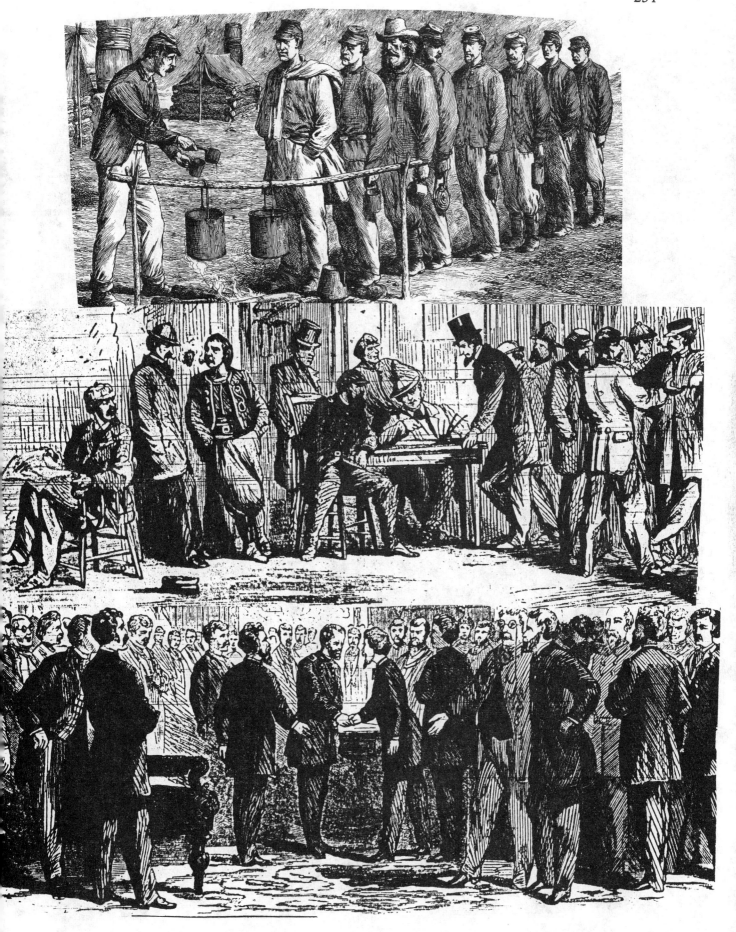

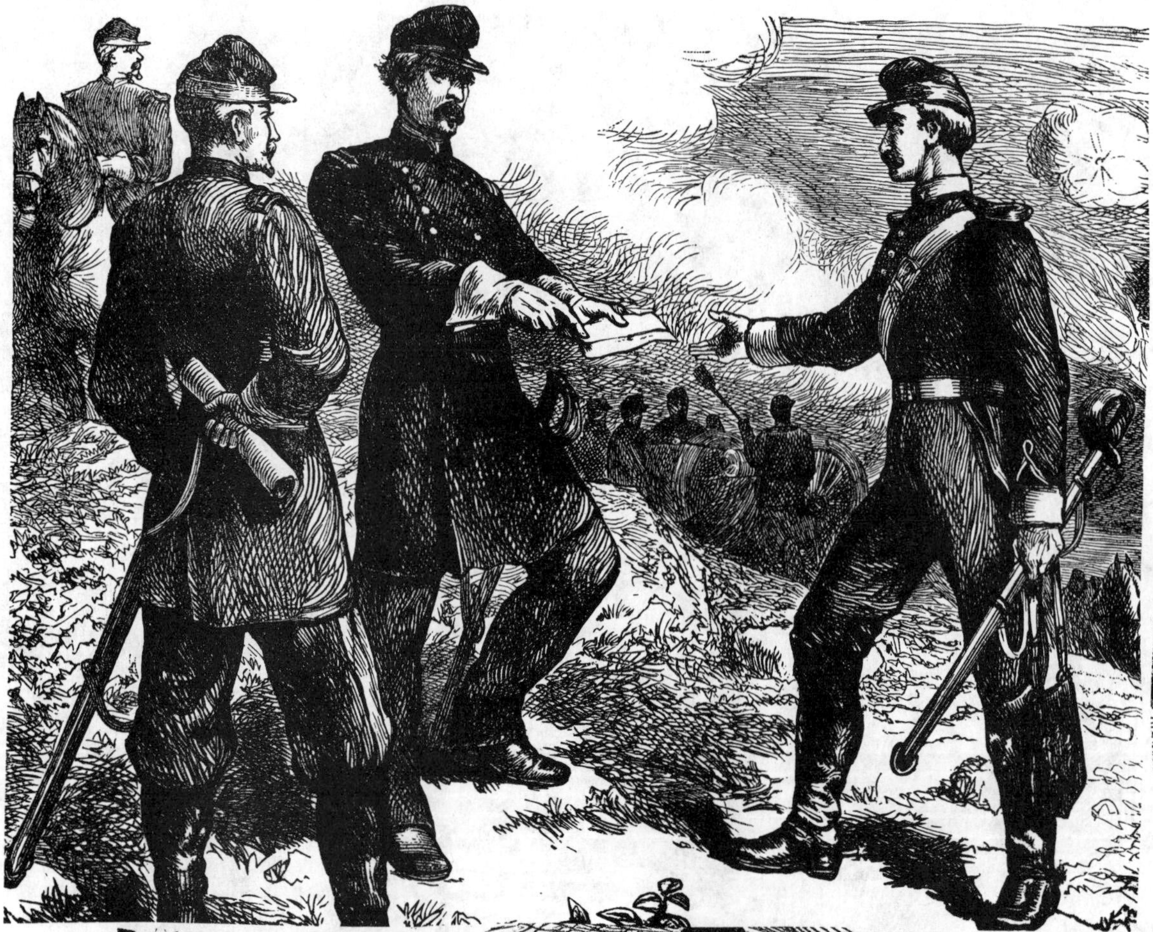

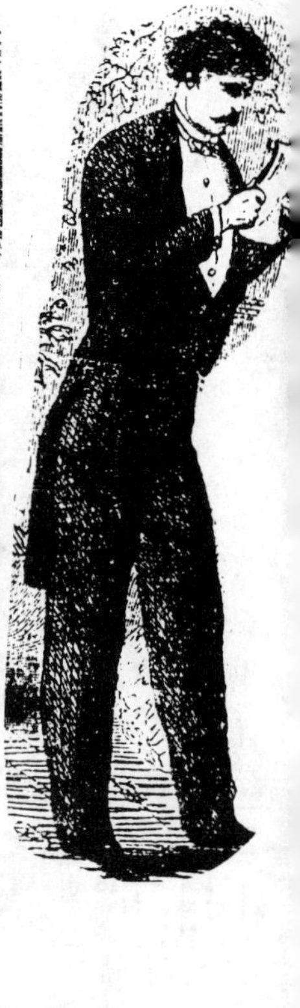

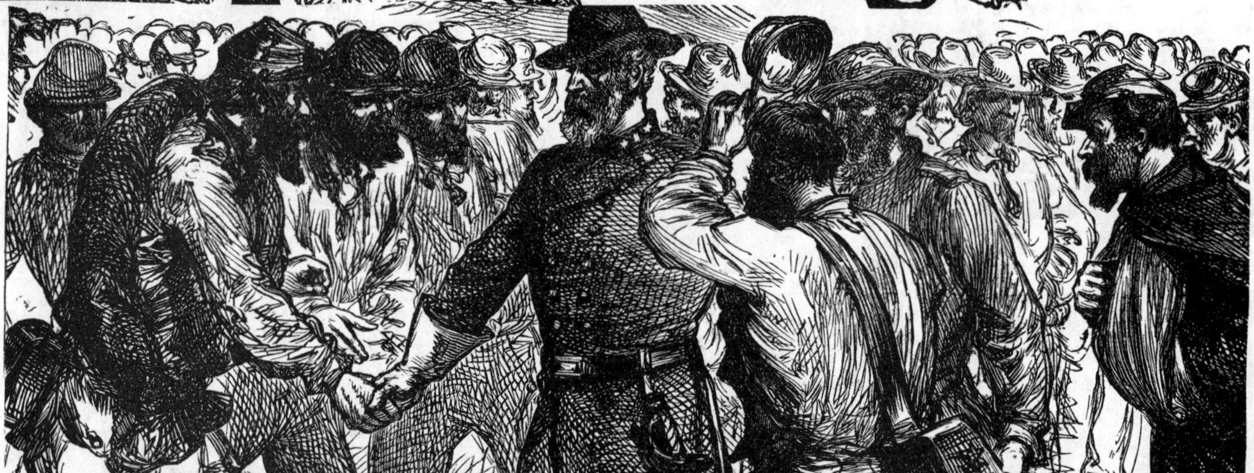

BIBLIOGRAPHY

American Heritage History of the Confident Years: 1865–1916. 1987

Angle, Paul & Davis, W. *Pictorial History of the Civil War Years.* 1985

Batterberry, Michael & Ariane. *Fashion: Mirror of History.* 1982

Barton, Lucy. *Historic Costume for the Stage.* 1961

Blair, M. *The Paisley Shawl.* 1904

Blum, Andre. *Historie du Costume: Les Modes au XIX Siecle.* 1930

Bowers, Michael. *North American Fighting Uniforms.* 1985

Bradley, C. *Western World Costume.* 1954

Brooke, I. *English Costume of the 19th Century.* 1977

Buck, Anne. *Victorian Costume & Costume Accessories.* 1984

Burgess, Janet. *Clothing Guidelines for the Civil War Era.* 1985

Byrde, P. *The Male Image.* 1979

Calasibetta, Charlotte. *Fairchild's Dictionary of Fashion.* 1975

Civil War Era Etiquette: Martine's Handbook & Vulgarisms in Conversation. 1866/1988

Civil War Ladies: Fashion & Needle-Arts of the Early 1860s. 1987

Contini, Mila. *Fashion: From Ancient Egypt to the Present Day.* 1965

Cooke, J, et al. *History's Timeline.* 1981

Cunnington, C.W. & P.E. & Beard, C. *A Dictionary of English Costume 900-1900.*

Davis, William. *Memorabilia of the Civil War.* 1991

Devere, Louis. *The Handbook of Practical Cutting on the Centre Point System.* 1866/1986

Earle, Alice. *Two Centuries of Costume in America.* 1903/1974

Estvan, Bela. *Pictures from the South.* 1863/1974

Faust, Patricia. *Historical Times Illustrated Encyclopedia of the Civil War.* 1986

Foster, Vanda. *Visual History of Costume: The 19th Century.* 1984

Giles, Edward. *The Art of Cutting & The History of English Costume.* 1887/1987

Hartley, Florence. *The Ladies' Hand Book of Fancy & Ornamental Work.* 1859/1991

Hayworthwaite, Philip. *Uniforms of the American Civil War.* 1985

Howell, Edgar. *United States Army Headgear 1855–1902.*

Johnson, David. *Uniform Buttons, American Armed Forces 1784–1948.* 1948

Kannik, P. & Carman, W. (ed.) *Military Uniforms in Color.* 1968

Katcher, Philip. *The American Soldier: U.S. Armies in Uniform 1755 to the Present.* 1990

Langelier, J.P. *Parade Ground Soldiers: Military Uniforms & Headress 1837–1910.* 1978

Lister, Kathleen. *Historic Costume.* 1942

Lloyd, Mark. *Combat Uniforms of the Civil War.* 1990

Lord, Francis. *Civil War Collector's Encyclopedia.* 1975/1984

McAfee, Michael & Etting, J. *Military Uniforms in America: Long Endure. The Civil War Period 1852–1867.* 1982

McAfee, Michael. *Zouave...The First & The Bravest.* (Exhibit cat.) 1979

McClellan, Elizabeth. *Historic Dress in America.* 1904

Minister, Edward. *The Complete Guide to Practical Cutting.* 1853/1993

Official Atlas of the Civil War. 1958

Ordnance Manual for the Use of Officers of the U.S. Army. 1841

Ordnance Manual for the Use of Officers of the U.S. Army. 1850

Ordnance Manual for the Use of Officers of the U.S. Army. 1862

Payne, Blanch. *History of Costume.* 1965

Peterson, Harold. *The American Sword 1775–1945.* 1954

Peterson, Mendel. *American Army Epaulets 1814–1872.*

Photographic History of the Civil War. 1957

Picken. M.B. *The Language of Fashion.* 1939

Ratti, A. et al. *Ratti and Paisley.* (Exhibit Cat.) 1987

Regulations for the Uniform & Dress of the Army of the United States. 1851

Schuyler, Hartley & Graham. *Illustrated Catalog of Civil War Military Goods.* 1864/1985

Scott, H.L. *Civil War Military Dictionary.*

Sichel, Marion. *Costume Reference #6: The Victorians.* 1978

Thomas, Michael. *A Confederate Sketchbook.* 1980

Todd, Frederick. *American Military Equipage 1851–1872.* 1977

Todd, Frederick & Krodel, F. *Soldiers of the American Army 1775–1954.* 1954

Uniforms of the Army of the United States 1774 to 1889.

Waugh, Norah. *The Cut of Men's Clothes 1600–1900.* 1964

Wilcox, R.T. *Five Centuries of American Costume.* 1963

Winter, Janet & Schultz, C. *Victorian Clothing 1840–1865.* 1980

Worrell, Estelle. *American Costume: 1840–1920.* 1929

Titles published by R.L. Shep

- ART OF CUTTING & HISTORY OF ENGLISH COSTUME (1887)
  by Edward Giles.

  THE BOOK OF COSTUME: or Annals of Fashion (1846)
  by The Countess of Wilton. Annotated Edition.

- CIVIL WAR ERA ETIQUETTE: Martine's Handbook & Vulgarisms
  in Conversation.

- CIVIL WAR LADIES: Fashions & Needle-Arts of the Early 1860's
  from *Peterson's Magazine 1861 & 1864* + hair styles & hair jewelry
  from Campbell's *Self-Instructor in the Art of Hair Work* 1867.

  DRESS & CLOAK CUTTER: Women's Costumes 1877-1882
  by Charles Hecklinger. Rev & Enlarged Edition.

- THE HANDBOOK OF PRACTICAL CUTTING on the Centre Point System
  (1866) by Louis Devere.

  THE LADIES GUIDE TO NEEDLE WORK (1877) by S. Annie Frost.

  THE LADIES' SELF INSTRUCTOR in Millinery & Mantua Making,
  Embroidery & Applique (1853).

  EDWARDIAN LADIES' TAILORING: The Twentieth Century System of
  Ladies' Garment Cutting (1910) by J.D. Hopkins.

  TAILORING OF THE BELLE EPOQUE: Vincent's Systems of Cutting all
  kinds of Tailor-Made Garments (1903) by W.D.F. Vincent.

  LATE GEORGIAN COSTUME: The Tailor's Friendly Instructor (1822)
  by J. Wyatt + The Art of Tying the Cravat (1828) by H. Le Blanc.

- THE LADIES' HAND BOOK OF FANCY & ORNAMENTAL WORK -
  Civil War Era - by Florence Hartley.

  EDWARDIAN HATS: The Art of Millinery (1909) by Mme. Anna Ben-Yusuf.

  CIVIL WAR COOKING: The Housekeeper's Encyclopedia
  by Mrs. E. F. Haskell.

- THE COMPLETE GUIDE TO PRACTICAL CUTTING (1853)
  by Edward Minister & Son.

  FREAKS OF FASHION: The Corset & The Crinoline (1868)
  by William Berry Lord.

  ART IN DRESS (1922) by P. Clement Brown.

  CORSETS: A Visual History.

  VICTORIAN NEEDLE-CRAFT: Artistic & Practical.

For more information and prices, write to:
R.L. Shep. Box 668. Mendocino, CA 95460 USA